TIGER HEART

TIGER HEART

My unexpected adventures
to make a difference in Darjeeling,
and what I learned about fate, fortitude,
and finding family . . . half a world away

Katrell Christie
Shannon McCaffrey

Health Communications, Inc.
Deerfield Beach, Florida

www.hcibooks.com

Library of Congress Cataloging-in-Publication Data
is available through the Library of Congress

© 2015 Katrell Christie and Shannon McCaffrey

ISBN-13: 978-07573-1858-0 (Paperback)
ISBN-10: 07573-1858-4 (Paperback)
ISBN-13: 978-07573-1859-7 (ePub)
ISBN-10: 07573-1859-2 (ePub)

Publisher: Health Communications, Inc.
3201 S.W. 15th Street
Deerfield Beach, FL 33442–8190

Cover art © Ryan Eschenbach
Cover design by Larissa Hise Henoch
Interior design and formatting by Lawna Patterson Oldfield

If you've ever taught me in school,
babysat me, held the door open for me,
let me borrow your pen in the checkout line,
been my camp counselor, bought me a drink,
cut my hair, not given me a parking ticket,
served me in a restaurant, listened to me complain,
given me a job, not hit me playing Roller Derby
when you probably should have, gone out dancing
with me, bought a coffee from me,
dry-cleaned my clothes, interned for the Learning Tea,
helped with the Learning Tea, helped me get a
buddy pass, gone to India with me, supported the
Learning Tea, or married me on a fishing boat
in the Mekong River, you are part of this
journey and have gotten me to this point.
Thank you for all of your support.

Contents

Coauthor's Note

I first met Katrell Christie in March 2014. My daughter's Girl Scout troop was studying India. The troop leader, a good friend, had heard of the work Katrell was doing to educate young women there, so we planned a mom's night out at her tea shop.

Katrell was in India on that first visit, but I loved the cozy, eccentric vibe of her shop at once. Long communal tables are punctuated with threadbare armchairs. Colorful Asian parasols dangle upside down from the ceiling. Books spill from the tall shelves.

Even as I was eating my dal and making small talk, I was sketching out a story pitch for the *Atlanta Journal-Constitution*, where I work as a reporter. When I finally met Katrell, I asked about tagging along to India on her next visit. I expected she'd welcome the publicity—a big spread in her hometown paper. Instead, she took some convincing. She knew the project needed publicity to thrive, but she gets uncomfortable in the spotlight. Nonetheless, after a little cajoling, I was invited along. The trip turned into a two-part story in the Atlanta paper. But, even so, it felt like there was more to say, this time in Katrell's own voice.

When we sat down to write this memoir, Katrell had a few conditions. She wanted to show her mistakes. She wanted to protect the young women in her project. They attend schools and a few students have Internet access, which allows their schoolmates to search anything that's written about them. We've shielded their identities in this book by changing their names. And she wanted to make sure she didn't exaggerate her role in any way. Many of the stories in the book were adapted from real-time posts she wrote in a private blog she's kept off and on over the years for close friends.

Other seemingly incredible tales are backed up by photos taken by the trusty Nikon that is her constant traveling companion. (I was skeptical when she described seeing a monkey catching a ride on the back of a mama pig with piglets, but, sure enough, there was a picture!)

We have also changed a few names to protect folks who live privately and never expected that their exploits would show up on a bookshelf somewhere. The timeline for some events has been condensed, but these are true tales from a life fully lived.

I have traveled to India with Katrell twice now. So what grand discovery have I made? In a way, I'm still processing the whole experience nearly a year later. And maybe that is my gift from India. That what I saw there has been woven deeply into the way I view the world. I've also come away with the knowledge that one person's life can take the most unlikely of detours and make a difference in the most unlikely of ways.

Shannon McCaffrey
March 2015

Chapter 1

THREE WISHES

"I slept and dreamt that life was joy.
I awoke and saw that life was service.
I acted and behold, service was joy."

—Rabindranath Tagore

he Indian defense minister wants to see you. Be here in twenty minutes."

The voice on the phone makes clear there is only one answer.

Moments later I am up and shivering, rummaging through my luggage in the dark, tugging on my least dirty kurta, and twisting my hair into one of those fake bun makers I'd bought at Walgreens. When one of the most powerful men in India requests your presence, you don't ask for time to dillydally. I'm thankful that on this trip I remembered to pack something other than my navy blue combat boots.

At the appointed hour, I'm sitting in a wicker chair perched on the side of a mountain on the terrace of the Windamere, Darjeeling's most opulent hotel. Fuchsia bougainvillea spills over a green lattice outdoor trellis and the snowcapped Himalaya Mountains are splayed out in front of us. I can see K2 between the clouds. We are ringed by a circle of staunch, beefy men with thick moustaches. Their uniforms are crisply pressed. They are all armed with AK-47s.

I am about to have tea.

Before I sit down, three immaculately dressed lawyers give me precise instructions on how to behave.

"You have ten minutes. Don't be foolish enough to actually order anything. You are not allowed to ask for food, even if the waiter offers. His assistant orders your tea. Do not even think about a second cup. After ten minutes, you are out of here; get up, thank him graciously, and ask to be excused."

I am half expecting them to ask me to pee in a cup or, at the very least, give me a pat down. In front of a lattice arbor dripping with flowers, they pat me down.

Then, the last in this group of lawyers tosses in a postscript: I am, he says, allowed to ask for three wishes.

"You know what you want, right?" he asks casually. His hands are clasped tightly and he gives me a head bobble and a curt smile.

"Um, uh, yeah. Sure."

It's early. I haven't had any caffeine. I'm hungry and I've had no time to prepare. I'm covered in sweat after running through town. I'd hurdled women roasting corn over hot coals on the ground and dodged dogs and roaming monkey families all while wearing a fancy kurta and some weird, crappy, lightweight rubber wedges I had purchased for a "what if" moment like this. I had taken the stairs two at a time up the switchback path that led to this hotel on a hill, and I'm still trying to get my head on straight.

I didn't know I was supposed to *ask* for anything. I thought we were going to get to know each other. Talk politics. Swap backstories.

Banter over what makes Georgia clay red. Compare our favorite desserts. Discuss world issues. Not wishes. But I also realized this might be the break I need.

※

My name is Katrell Christie, and I was named after my dad's favorite hardware store.

How I've come to be sipping tea in this place, half a world away from my home in Atlanta, is part of the strange patchwork of tales that make up my life.

A sampling:

- I skated competitive Roller Derby under the alias Takillya Sunrise.
- I once made my living tromping around Italy buying art for a client.
- I spent part of my childhood growing up in government project housing.
- I opened a tea shop, even though I really prefer coffee.
- I watched my favorite uncle die of AIDS.
- I have big hair, a big butt, and big boobs.
- I clogged with Billy Bob's peewee cloggers.
- I was held up by a pregnant wanderer in Paris.
- My mom was diagnosed with stage-four brain cancer.
- For ten-plus years, I kept a weekly dinner date with a flamboyant, fantastic, and very sarcastic gay man.
- I own more than five hundred vintage costumes that were gifted to me.
- And, on a restless whim, I took a trip to India.

In India, what was supposed to be a spontaneous jaunt turned my life in a new direction after I crossed paths with three painfully shy teenage girls at a Buddhist orphanage in Darjeeling. When I learned they were going to be put out on the street once they turned seventeen, I reached the simple conclusion that I couldn't walk away.

There was no grand plan. When I flew to India for the first time, I was not-so-secretly wishing I'd gone to drink margaritas at some beach in Florida instead. I did have a vague idea that I might be able to link my small Atlanta tea shop to an education project in Darjeeling, where my tea came from. But I had no clue that one day I would be responsible for a houseful of female college students.

They are some of India's forgotten girls. And it's quite likely they could've been sex trafficked, earned a living carrying bricks on their backs, or become domestic servants. Some of them might've disappeared completely without anyone to look for them or care where they went.

Let me say this right away: There are a lot of amazing people out there who are doing far more to help than I can ever hope to. I am in awe of them. I'm also here to tell you that I have had some pretty spectacular failures along the way. Big, embarrassing screwups. And I have been disappointed by people who promise to help but only seem interested in following through when someone is watching. Other times, I have been surprised by complete wildcards who have stepped up to the plate just because it was the right thing to do.

A lot of people out there are looking for happiness. They buy books and meditate and get facelifts and occasionally drink lots of wine. What I've found is that sometimes you can also find true meaning and contentment by looking outward and focusing your energy on helping someone else.

For me, I'm just doing what I can. There is no real solution but to try my best every day and hope I can make some positive change somewhere—even for one second. Having someone smile when they weren't or knowing that those young women aren't begging on the streets at this moment is an accomplishment and a solution in the right now. I can't save the world, and I might not make an earthshaking difference outside of one isolated town, but I am changing the lives of these particular young women forever with the help and resources I have collected from my mentors. You never know who these young women will become. They have a wide path ahead of them, and I know they are going to do amazing things. Great leaders come from everyday people and all villains and heroes have a moment to decide which side they are on or who they are fighting for.

If there is one thing my life has taught me, it's that sometimes you just have to lean into the curve and let go. Life is pretty fantastic if you let it take you where it wants you to be . . . which is how I have come to be sitting on a hotel terrace with one of the most powerful men in India. It's one of those "only in India" stories.

※

The night before I "crashed" a meeting of the Darjeeling Rotary Club. Back in Atlanta, my diverse club includes men and women from Liberia, Pakistan, and Egypt, as well as civil rights leaders who once marched alongside Dr. Martin Luther King Jr. But as

I walked into this club, I noticed right away that diversity wasn't their strong suit. This group was composed of all men, not a woman in the house. They were lined up stiffly at a long banquet table, like a Harry Potter luncheon.

The meeting was held in a dimly lit hotel basement. Dark wood covered the walls and ceiling, and a few dusty Tibetan tapestries hung haphazardly from the wood paneling. I settled in. Some late-arriving members rushed in and did a stumbling, head-swiveling, neck-breaking double take. The record scratched as they stared at the white, blond-haired woman who'd invaded their man cave.

Two shot glasses were slammed down in front of each of us, filled to the rim with Johnny Walker Black. The men watched me curiously. They leaned down against the table and hoisted the first shot, in what was obviously a premeeting ritual. I smiled, gamely threw back my own, and stifled a stomach-churning grimace.

The men followed with a gulp of water as a chaser. But I wasn't going near suspect water. Breathing deeply through my nose and trying to keep my face composed, I let the whiskey burn its way down to my gut. Shot two. Same drill. It hurt, but I had passed the test. With some looks of astonishment and admiration, they kindly adopted me into their circle.

I told them all about my project in their hometown, the Learning Tea, and they were eager to help. As I doled out business cards at the end of the meeting, one of the Rotarians, wrapped up in a Nepali wool scarf, mentioned in passing that the Indian defense minister was in town.

"He is a very powerful and influential man in India. Would you like to meet him?"

"Sure, why not?" I replied. I quickly sorted this into the already full "unlikely to ever happen" category and forgot about it—until my phone rang very early the next morning.

Which brings me back to the Windamere, where tea is about to be served.

❈

By the time I reach the great man, I feel like I'm being shot out of a cannon. He has a soft, kind face and is wearing a beautiful, perfectly tailored, long, gold kurta. He is sitting in a wingback wicker chair next to a short wicker table and another wicker chair, where one of his aides indicates I should sit. Two of his aides are sitting in smaller chairs behind him, and behind them, surrounding us in a semicircle, are the soldiers. We are facing each other, and to our left is a green metal railing where the earth drops off a cliff to a valley of barely visible small villages below. The view is stunning, with misty clouds slowly rolling in like dragon's breath through the Himalayas.

The defense minister is balancing a porcelain cup and saucer of tea on one knee and greets me with a soft smile. I sit down and start talking. And talking. I tell him about me and my project and my girls. I am like a live auctioneer, going and going at warp speed. I'm selling it with everything I have. I keep eye contact going to see if he breaks with disinterest. He listens calmly. And when I run out of breath, he contemplates the sky.

That's the thing about Indians. They are completely okay with dead air. They will pause and consider something for an excruciatingly long moment before talking. This is extremely unnerving for Americans. We are hell-bent on filling every nook and cranny of silence.

I bounce my knee with nervousness and hold my breath in expectation of his coming words. I am leaning forward, biting my lip, waiting for his next move. When he finally speaks, it's a Yoda-like poetic riddle. The answer comes before the question.

"Darjeeling," he says. Then he gazes at the sky. His aides, obviously used to this, also stare off into space. Then, just as I think he has nodded off, he asks, "The clouds and the sky. Are there words?"

We continue talking. When the waiter stops by and asks if I would like more tea, I shake my head fervently and immediately decline, remembering the very specific orders of my minder. The defense minister considers me for a moment and determines, with a smile, that, yes, I will have a second cup of tea. I feel the aides glance at each other in my periphery, and I can tell by the way they twitch that this doesn't happen often.

We talk about politics and the puzzle that is India, and then he pauses. I notice he has remarkably gentle eyes. His kind, slow hand gestures remind me of tai chi. I can hear birds chirping through the wind. A small spider inches his way across the stone patio floor. It seems like hours tick by.

Then he asks what my wish is. The big question. I'd scrambled to come up with my list as I paced back and forth behind the flowering trellis before the meeting.

I hear myself rattle off my three finalists: space in an unused government building that we might be able to use as a Learning Tea center, seats in the nursing school for the girls, and access to any scholarships they might be eligible for.

One bushy eyebrow inches skyward.

"How much," he asks, "does it cost to educate one girl for a year?"

I do some quick math in my head.

When I cough up a figure, without hesitation he writes a check from his personal account.

As I prepare to leave, he hands me a small piece of paper folded into an even smaller square.

"This is my home address in Delhi," he says. "If you are there, please visit me."

Chapter 2

FOLLOW THE ORANGE

> "To live will be an awfully
> big adventure."
>
> —J. M. Barrie, *Peter Pan*

 chose the name of my tea shop—Dr. Bombay's Underwater Tea Party—because it sounded whimsical. India wasn't a part of the equation. Not even remotely. It had never even crossed my mind. I didn't do yoga. I had no deep yearning to see the Taj Mahal or tour Hindu temples. I didn't harbor some spiritual desire to follow the path of the Buddha.

But one day, a regular customer, Cate, walks into my shop raving about a trip she took there as a Rotary Club scholar. She's planning to go again, and her enthusiasm is infectious.

"You should come," she says, after breezing in. "It will be fun."

"Girl, if I go on vacation, I'm going to Florida, to the beach, to throw a book over my head and drink margaritas for breakfast. India? No thanks."

"No, really," she persists. "I think you'd love it; it's wonderful. Plus, I need your help."

I don't give it much thought. Me going to India for three months, as required by the Rotary project, seems about as likely to happen as me suddenly deciding to peel and eat a raw onion. As a new business owner, my work stretches as far as I can see. Days off? What are those?

But Cate's friendly, low-key lobbying continues on her frequent visits. She brings me fresh-baked cookies and little jelly jars of homemade chai. She shows me photos of her in front of the Taj Mahal or smiling wildly while hanging out of a moving train. I soak up colorful saris, the desert of rolling hills, and camels adorned in red and blue headdresses.

The small group she will be traveling with begins to hold their planning meetings at my shop. And the idea gradually begins to take root as my stress level mounts. In the space of a few days, I have to fire an employee for stealing and another one quits to return to college. I'm spent, burned out, and working all their shifts. I want a break, a place where I can collect my thoughts and stop debating about how I got myself into this mess.

The next time Cate walks into the shop, she skips up to the counter with an inquiring expression, and I surprise myself.

"Okay. I'll go."

I have a vague idea that I can see where my tea comes from and maybe provide a little help to someone along the way. Cate promises me a free place to stay for some of the trip and a world of adventure. Managing to poach a generous friend's Delta buddy pass, suddenly I am heading halfway around the world. It's the first time I've been away from my shop since I opened it about three years earlier.

※

As my plane touches down in Mumbai, I can see the teetering jumble of slums next to the airport, houses made from corrugated metal and blue tarps. Entering the city of twelve million people, I feel almost breathless with panic. It's not what I expected: the overwhelming smell of incense, livestock, and diesel fuel; the heat; the constantly blaring car horns; and the press of so many people.

I'm planning to meet up with Cate in Hyderabad in a few days, but for now I'm on my own with almost no idea of what to do. What I do know is that I want out of here.

Nervously flipping open my *Lonely Planet* guidebook, I stop in the middle to look through the photo pages. One shows the Golden Temple in Amritsar. Another is a cluster of cows roaming busy streets in Kolkata. Then there's a beach town dressed up for a festival. But I'm drawn to one mysterious photo showing pink tur-reted buildings and stone steps descending into the Ganges River.

This place looks like nothing I've ever seen. It's Varanasi, the holiest site in the Hindu religion and one of the oldest cities on the planet. It seems like as good a plan as any. I can hide out there for some R&R until I meet up with Cate.

Cranking some Dinosaur Jr. on my iPod to calm my nerves, I hop on a train and plunge into the heart of the Indian countryside in search of the picture.

Nine hundred miles later, in the middle of the night, I arrive at a tiny, threadbare hotel.

As my little tuk-tuk rolls to a stop, I see the staff is sleeping outside on the stairs. Some are curled around the potted plants surrounding the front of the building. Others are stretched out in the lobby on the hard floor. They suddenly jump up and grab my bags.

I'm jet-lagged and disoriented. The hotel owner senses my confusion and takes pity. "We just had a last-minute cancellation," he says. "Welcome."

As he deposits me in my room, I ask him for tips on local sites and he offers me some advice.

"Before dawn," he says, "follow the orange."

And so, just a few hours later, I find myself back out in front of my hotel, exhausted and dizzy, without any notion, really, about what to make of his cryptic advice. Peering down the dark dirt street, under a hazy streetlight off in the distance, I can see a man far ahead in an orange turban and a traditional orange robe.

I do as I was told. Quietly trailing after the man through the dark, I pick my way around sleeping dogs, sleeping cows, and a couple of sleeping families cuddled up on blankets. I am a clueless pilgrim winding through the narrow streets of the ancient city.

As the moon lights the way, we are joined by a growing crowd. Everyone is walking in silence. Following the moving mass, I am swept up in a sea of orange, quietly shuffling down long corridors, up broken stairs, and back down through narrow alleyways. Once or twice I am straddling a goat or climbing around a sleeping bull that is blocking the path, but I keep moving with the crowd.

The walk, which seems like hours, rounds a sharp corner. A small sliver of morning blue light peeks through an opening in a building entryway. I walk through it and everything opens up. The sights and sounds hit me square in the face, and I work to adjust my eyes.

The Ganges River runs as far as I can see in either direction. It is flat and wide with nothing on the other side. Calm and gray, it looks like a sheet of paper with barely any ripples. Long, skinny boats are scattered off the shore. I see one with about twenty men lined from end to end, all wearing bright orange turbans.

This river is a goddess, the mother, a spiritual life force, I had read in my *Lonely Planet* guidebook on the train, and bathing in it is known to be purifying. I had also read on the plane that in the Hindu religion, they believe that if you die in Varanasi, your soul will be released from the reincarnation cycle and you will attain spiritual liberation.

I see people pouring out of each opening in the buildings that lead down to the water. The steep steps—known as ghats—line the river like ancient bleachers built to view the show. Some of them are crumbling but most are still intact.

I carefully make my way down to the river.

"Boat ride, madam?"

At first I shake my head no as a man offers up his small, blue wooden boat. But he follows me down a few broken steps, and I can make out the thousands of people in my view. The crowd is a living, breathing mass, and I feel claustrophobic. The river looks like an escape.

"Okay. Let's go."

I shove a small wad of rupees into his weather-beaten hand. He helps me into the boat and rows out onto the relative calm of the Ganges, where I can watch the hordes of devout worshippers flow into the river from what seems like a safe distance.

It's a surreal scene. Prayers blare from loudspeakers. Indian women in vivid saris stand in the water up to their waists yelling at the sky, supposedly to scare away a demon that can snatch up unborn children. The air is thick with the ashy smell of charred remains from funeral pyres blazing on the cremation ghats dotting the bottom steps in some parts of the river. Little bits of ashes catch in my breath and float in the wind like snowflakes.

I hear dogs barking, goats bleating, and crows screeching as they circle us overhead. Every ten steps or so, someone is beating a drum louder than the last. There is a lady singing on a loudspeaker in a high-pitched voice. Eerie wailing rises up within the heat and the haze of the blaring sunrise. The sound fills every inch of space like smoke.

I have finally caught my breath when darkness begins to blot out the morning light. A storm seems to be fast approaching. The last place I want to be in bad weather is in the middle of the river in this wonkity little boat.

I turn to the boat owner and plead, "Excuse me, sir, please take me back to shore."

He smiles and waggles his head from side to side in the good-natured, noncommittal way that Indians do. It can mean yes or no or just "hmm" depending on the context. In this moment, it causes frustration, which quickly turns into fear.

I look for an opening in the crowd for us to dock but see none. The wall of people stretches both ways for miles.

The sky blackens and I start to see the soft white clouds turn silver with darkness. The shade and the shadows inch their way across the river to my boat.

"Please, now. Take me back to shore. *Now.*"

My terror is lost on this man, who apparently speaks only Hindi.

I imagine myself drowning in this river half a world away from home.

My fear is consuming. I begin to sweat and think of all the things I have yet to do. I think about my family, my friends, my dogs, my little tea shop. I think about the e-mail I forgot to send yesterday, that my itinerary had a diversion.

The clouds get darker, and even though I know how to swim, I know I will surely drown in my fight for the shoreline.

I am trying to talk myself into calm but it's not working. I am about ready to lunge at him and grab the oars myself when the boatman finally, through jumbled sentences, utters a single word that I actually understand: "eclipse."

It is July 22, 2009, and I am witnessing the longest-lasting total solar eclipse in a century. Varanasi is one of a handful of spots on the planet—a slice across Asia—where this can even be seen.

I could've chosen hundreds of other destinations, but by complete chance I've blundered upon the holiest Hindu city in India on the day of a mystical eclipse.

The noise from the bank hushes into complete silence as six minutes and thirty-nine seconds tick by in complete darkness. And here I float on the Ganges River in the dark, with only the sound of tiny waves lapping against the boat.

Chapter 3

"PROJECT NO GOOD"

"Everything must go."

—Buddhist proverb

 few days after the eclipse, I prepare to leave Varanasi to meet up with Cate. I opt to have my small lot of clothes laundered. This is before I understand that, in India, the bucket in the bathroom doubles as the washing machine. I head to the café on the hotel roof to take a few panoramic photos. Meandering through the groups of people, toward the balcony, I see my clothes hanging on the backs of the chairs drying. My underwear and bras are blowing loosely in the wind.

After one plane flight, a few bus rides, and one short tuk-tuk ride, I arrive in Hyderabad. Cate will be waiting near the Charminar, a large marble monument that sits in the city center. Compared to the rich, spicy hues of Varanasi, Hyderabad is stark and minimal. Buildings in this predominantly Muslim city are bleached white. Women move through the dry, dusty streets in full, billowing burqas. The call to prayer echoes throughout the city, regular as clockwork.

As I climb off the bus, I stop cold. Two women are walking together, the younger one leading the older one along by the arm. The older woman's eyes meet mine and I instinctively draw back. Her face is missing. Well, not missing exactly. But what is left of it is a slick of scarred skin. Her nose and her mouth are just small holes. An acid attack. An old one from the look of it. I had heard about these attacks on women. This is so unthinkable to me it's hard to process.

I meet up with Cate. She is standing on the side of the road, waving her arm to grab my attention but it's her ten-gallon smile I see first. Tall and blond, she is easy to spot. Cate went to Spelman College, Atlanta's historically black school for women, and is now studying to be a human rights lawyer. She is one of those strong women who has the ability to make anyone feel comfortable and is always right there in the moment with you. She is kind to the core but is no pushover. I think people are drawn to familiarity, to slightly different versions of themselves. This is definitely true with Cate and me. Although she's younger than me (and nicer), I have always felt like she is the wise, steady one.

Cate's handicraft project is working to help market the pearls that have made Hyderabad famous. The region's specialty is drilling tiny holes in the ivory orbs so they can be strung into necklaces. We are trying to help women here create a sustainable business, teaching them to open a bank account, finding the materials they need, and even involving their husbands in selling the finished product.

The two of us are bunking in a deserted college dorm. It's a stark but beautiful oasis in the middle of this dusty, dry city. The furnishings inside are minimal but the garden is magical. Bougainvillea creeps up the sides of the building and little gravel paths lead to an outdoor pagoda covered in colorful tile. It's the most vegetation I have seen in this town.

One day there's a report of a cobra in the building—an Indian cobra with the fanned-out hood, the same kind that is summoned out of a basket by a flute. Our local hosts say it's curled up under a desk on the first floor. My room is on the first floor. I change rooms.

They also tell me—with the same intensity as "pass the potatoes"—that some species of cobras can grow up to eighteen feet long and can stand up to five feet tall. When they are ready to strike, they spit in the eyes of their prey and blind them. If they bite you, you die. Your heart stops. There's no way you can get to the hospital in time.

While I find the thought of a snake unsettling, our morning alarm is the call to prayer broadcast by speakers all over the city, which I find very peaceful. At each respective hour of prayer, the call to the faithful can be heard throughout the city.

Every morning we take a cold shower from a bucket that is delivered to our room, and then we head down the dusty path that leads to the main road from the college. "When you see a bus, start running," Cate tells me. "This isn't an official stop." When the bus draws near, we run alongside it and yell to the driver, asking him in which direction he's heading. If it's ours, we speed up and jump in the door. The bus never actually stops. At night, when we return to the dorm, there are only men on the bus. I wear my blond hair pulled back tight with a scarf that covers my head and most of my face. Cate and I sit in the back of the bus. It doesn't matter. The men sit facing backward in their seats, openly staring at us.

After a bumpy, forty-five-minute bus ride, we catch a tuk-tuk, which brings us to our final destination. Almost. Most tuk-tuk drivers won't go the last few blocks because it's considered a dangerous neighborhood.

At the workroom, Cate and I string pearls with a group of local women all day. As we work, I watch the women. Some shed their heavy coverings when they enter the workroom, but others remain fully covered, with only a glimpse of their eyes visible. It's disconcerting. I'm a Southern girl. My mother taught me to always smile at people when your eyes meet. But with these women—their faces cloaked—I get nothing back. I can't connect.

Even worse, I can't get my mind off the idea that no matter what these women do, they will never get off this impoverished path. I had never wrapped my brain around this reality until now, as I sit here, hour after hour, without a common word, stringing pearls— pearls that will be worn on a bare and lovely neck by some other woman with a dazzling smile and a bright future stretching out before her.

Slowly I begin to forge a connection with a few women in the program. One of them, Motavu, invites Cate and me to come to her home for dinner. I don't realize what a big deal this is until we show up.

We are her guests for puja, a celebration of one of the hundreds of Hindu deities. This particular one is for Lakshmi, the goddess of wealth.

Motavu is poor in a way that most Americans can't even imagine. Her house is a tiny two-room concrete structure about the size of a shed. It houses her husband, her mother, and her two daughters. They own one plastic chair, but everyone sits and sleeps on plastic mats covering the dirt floor.

The family has built a small altar for the occasion. Around it sit bowls of yogurt and a salad. Potent incense and candles are burning. They chant for about thirty minutes. They twirl the incense around in a circle and toss handfuls of rice and flowers at a picture of the goddess.

One of Motavu's daughters rubs yellow turmeric all over our feet. She makes us little bracelets with leaves tied to them and smears red dots on our foreheads, as well as yellow and orange stripes on our cheeks.

We drink a sweet, room-temperature substance that resembles curdled cottage cheese, which is poured into our hands. We are handed a leaf with a banana and a packet of sugar to put on the altar. It's all beautiful, but I have no idea what any of it means. I'm learning.

"How do you like my home?" Motavu asks, gesturing to the marigolds she's taped to the water-stained concrete walls for the occasion. She is visibly proud. I tell her that I think her home is beautiful. I am humbled by her kindness.

We sit on the floor while her neighbors parade by the open door to gawk, but it never feels intrusive; they are warm and hospitable, and welcome us with open arms. Cate and I are like unicorns who have suddenly materialized in the living room.

Motavu prepares a huge meal for the celebration, which is served on palm leaves. Cate and I sit on the floor and eat while her family watches. The room is too small for all of us to sit at the same time, so they stand and wait patiently until we are done before they eat their own meal. A crowd of neighbors clusters around the window and the doorway. There is a lot of anticipation from the eager crowd for the sound of "yum" every time we take a bite; a belly-rub motion promptly follows, and they look at one another and grin. Motavu smiles, shakes her head, and looks up at the ceiling with pride. When a new group takes its position to get a look, Motavu's family encourages more oohs and aahs out of us. This goes on for the entire meal and becomes more over the top and hilarious with each bite. Motavu loves the dramatic accolades.

After dinner, Motavu's husband sends his daughters to the store and they return with small packets of oil. He warms them up over a small propane tank and proceeds to give Cate and I hot oil scalp massages. (This results in turning my already big-ass hair into a gigantic haystack "do" that lasts for days with only cold water to bathe.)

The night is restorative. The meal is delicious. I'm moved to see how much Motavu's husband clearly adores her and their daughters and how giving they are with what little they have.

I fall hard for the Indian people, many of whom enjoy an uncomplicated happiness.

※

Before long, I'm volunteering at a school in Hyderabad, educating the children of the women stringing pearls. We Westerners are asked to lead a project with the kids. There are four of us; the two other ladies besides me and Cate are students from the University of Georgia. One woman brings a globe and makes maps to show the children where we live. Another purchases toothbrushes and teaches them about dental hygiene.

Most of the students don't get lunch on any given day. The classrooms are filled with frail children seated on the floor with red and blue plastic step stools for desks. I watch as some pull out small metal containers from their bags and eat. Other children just sit and play with their hands. I head to the market and purchase fruit for them, but I know it's just a temporary fix.

It's alarming and deeply disturbing watching tiny two- and three-year-olds go without. I remember all the food left on trays at my school lunchroom while growing up.

I ask the teachers about it, and they respond simply, "They are too poor; these families can't afford it."

After some thought, I have an idea for a project—to build raised garden boxes for the roof of their building. They can grow vegetables to eat for lunch and learn how to replant the seeds, giving them a sustainable food source.

To help me, I hire Zabeers, a driver I met at the train station. He is chunky and in his forties, with a big, thick mustache that covers the bottom half of his face. A day earlier, Cate and I had jumped into his and his brother's cab. When they dropped us off at the school, we proposed that he drive us for our entire time in Hyderabad.

"Your driver is waiting outside," I hear from Salika, the woman who works at the school.

I collect my things and head out the front door. There is Zabeers, lying in the grass.

"Okay, let's go," I say with a smile.

He doesn't understand, so I motion for us to head to the front of the building. We start circling the building, looking for his car. I make the motion of holding on to a steering wheel and he laughs. I'm following him; he is following me. After a few tours around the grounds, the college garden crew comes out to watch. I ask one of them to have Zabeers take me to his car. They chat for a few moments and then he tells me that I only asked for a driver, not a car, and that the cab is his brother's, not his.

By chance, one of the college staff members owns a tiny, beat-up Tata that he is willing to rent to me. Zabeers and I climb into the car and drive off to pick up the supplies.

He and I do not share even a single word in each other's language. The director of the school has to get on the phone to tell him what I'm looking for.

Zabeers and I do, however, figure out a primitive means of communicating. When I say, "Yay! Awesome!" and clap, and then he replies, "Yay! Vashom!" and claps, it means we are on the same page and heading in the right direction. At least I think it does. I start drawing pictures in a notebook of the things I need.

Our road trips are beyond sweaty; the back windows only roll halfway down and it's well over 100 degrees every day. Traffic here is terrible; most of the streets are made from blowing dirt, and there are so many people, we rarely make it above twenty miles per hour.

I wipe the steam from my glasses.

I see really insane things, but half of them are so ridiculous that my brain says to itself, *You can't handle this. . . . Let's pretend you didn't just see that. Move along; there is nothing to see here.*

The stores here look like U-Haul storage spaces, row after row of concrete square rooms completely open to the street. A typical block consists of five cell phone stores, a steaming samosa stand, a glittery sari store, a flip-flop store, and, of course, my favorite: a butcher's shop.

I'm a longtime vegetarian, so I am clearly not impartial here. I try to divert my eyes, but I still see a lot more than I want to. Legs and rib cages dangle from hooks in the hot sun, completely unrefrigerated. Sometimes there is a live goat tied up or a pile of chicken cages stuffed full of hens.

We're stopped in yet another traffic jam when I watch a man walk up and point to a pile of ground meat heaped on a scale. He looks at the butcher, who gestures to the price on the scale. The man shakes his head no. The butcher waves his hands around the mound of meat and a swarm of flies rises off of it like a dark cloud. The man looks at the scale again, shakes his head yes this time, and pays for the meat.

Trying to find supplies to make a garden, I quickly learn the challenges of shopping in India. There is no Home Depot. In fact, stores here don't even sell two related items. If you want to buy a hammer, you have to drive a mile away to a different store to find the nails.

We visit three locations in search of wood. Finally, we find used crates that I figure we can repurpose. But, naturally, they don't fit in the Tata, which is about the size of a VW Rabbit. I haven't seen any wood here, and these crates are too precious to leave, so I flag down a tuk-tuk driver. We haggle over the price for about twenty minutes in the middle of the road, and I finally convince him to deliver the crates to the school, hoping they actually get there. Zabeers tells the driver where to go, and at the end of the conversation, they both laugh, I'm assuming over the absurdity of it all—or maybe at me.

Next is the matter of finding dirt. How do you draw a bag of dirt? There is no brown or black soil here. It's either red dirt or sand. And it doesn't come in a bag on aisle nine. Nope. You shovel it yourself off the side of the road. Loaded down with a few big bags of red dirt, the hatchback of our borrowed Tata scrapes the ground. I can tell Zabeers is clueless about what he must think is a very strange tourist on a wild-goose chase, but he's getting paid and that makes him happy.

I manage to buy burlap bags, once used for shipping saris, to use as fabric to line the beds. They charge me about one dollar to basically dispose of their trash. Zabeers laughs.

For seeds, we drive an hour out of town only to find the store is closed for yet another Hindu god celebration day. The next day we repeat the journey and pick up seeds for tomatoes, okra, cucumbers, green bell peppers, beans, eggplant, and cabbage.

I borrow a hammer from the school. It consists of a piece of bamboo with a chunk of metal tied to the top.

Total time for retrieving supplies, in a non-air-conditioned car, in 100-degree heat with absolutely no real communication with the driver: about four days.

Zabeers has been giggling his way through these strange errands. I'm sure he is thinking, *Crazy American lady driving around buying trash and dirt, paying too much.*

But I feel good. Success.

The day of the project, Zabeers helps me gather all of the supplies I have piled up from the college grounds. I convince him to drive me to the address I had written down in Hindi. He is very suspicious of my destination, bouncing down the washed-out street to the school. I haul all the supplies out of the Tata. Zabeers watches me curiously from the front seat, leaning on the steering wheel as I walk in.

Seeing me opening one of our bags of dirt by the front door, he comes over to help me, probably thinking I am going to haul it back out to the car so he can drive my dirt around some more. I wave my hands no, trying to explain the method to my madness.

A little girl nearby steps in to help me translate, explaining what we are doing to Zabeers. I hear her say "gaaa-r-den," and then something in Hindi. She makes hand signals for something blooming. Then she mimes eating something. She and Zabeers exchange a few more words, and then I see Zabeers's eyes well up with tears. He smiles and nods at me as he walks back out to the car.

Excited to share my project with the kids, I head to the roof and arrange the crates and burlap sacks to hold the soil to let water run through. I line up the kids from the front door up two flights of stairs to the roof—fire brigade–style—to pass the soil in buckets.

"Stop. Project no good." It's a teacher, and she is waving her arms at me.

"Kids want to play games," she continues.

I assume there is a language barrier and we are lost in translation.

"I'm leaving in a few days," I tell her. "And I want to finish this."

"Tomorrow is a Hindu holiday," she informs me. "And that's followed by a Muslim holiday Thursday. And Friday school is closed."

I take a deep breath. I tell her it might be more important for the kids to learn about sustainable food sources. The fact that everyone would have a snack or lunch when the vegetables are grown should probably trump their game-playing for the rest of the afternoon.

She isn't having it.

"Project no good," she repeats.

Another teacher comes and tells the kids to go sit down.

"No family grow no vegetable," she says.

"Project no good. Be no mad. Project no good."

She shakes her head from side to side, which I can tell, in this case, means no.

I am completely frustrated. I am on my last pack of cigarettes in a town full of cigarette haters. There are cameras mounted to poles all around ready to catch me and slap me with a smoking ticket. The nearest bar is probably in Atlanta, and I have officially wasted the last four days.

But there is one more setback that will hit me even harder.

The room where we work on the pearls has a white floor. One day I see a pool of blood near one of the women working on the jewelry. Then I see drips of blood on the pearls she is working with. She is young and always wears a full burqa. Her mother is also in the group.

With a lot of detective work and questions, I find out that her father, who has worked for the local police force, is beating her and has been for some time. The blood is coming from fresh wounds on her back and arms.

All the anger that has been building in me about the way women are treated in this country explodes; I am pissed. Everything I'm accustomed to is totally ripped out from under me. The only way I can think of to deal with this is to find a way to get her out. I sure as hell would never stay in a situation like this. I spend hours bitching to Cate and trying to devise a plan. I contact an immigration lawyer back home. Can I get her a visa? Surely there is a domestic violence group that could help.

But before I get very far, she and her mother find me. The young woman tells me she doesn't want to leave. She can't leave. If she leaves, her father will undoubtedly turn his beatings on her younger siblings. She also can't accept the fact that leaving would be a betrayal to her community. She would never be welcomed back.

I am floored.

In my mind, I was offering help and there was no way she wouldn't take it. It would have been complicated, sure. But I hadn't contemplated that she wouldn't *want* help.

I realize how naive I was. I should never have approached the situation believing that she would be thankful for a chance to leave all she knew and strike out on her own.

But one thing emerges from this sad and frustrating episode. My idea to give back while I'm in India begins to take shape. The pieces come together. I resolve that I will help someone, a girl, ideally without a father to hold her back.

Chapter 4

LOOK ALIVE!

> "Why, sometimes I've believed
> as many as six impossible things
> before breakfast."
>
> —Lewis Carroll,
> *Alice in Wonderland*

was swinging back and forth, my feet high in the air.

I was four, small, and extremely pale with almost white hair. I had two giant cowlicks in the front of my hair and two larger ones in the back that gave me a natural Bumpit. My hair was always wild and out of control, kind of like me. I was small for my size and had a terrible Cindy Brady lisp that followed me into middle school (and that sometimes still reappears when I get nervous). "Sammy the snake swims swiftly through the grass."

My favorite uniform was a unitard with corduroy bell-bottoms and a pair of black-and-white saddle oxfords. I carried around a puppet of Fozzie from *The Muppet Show* and stuffed my valuables inside his chest. I had been shuffled around to different church day schools, Mommy's Day Out programs, and all the chain day cares Atlanta had to offer.

I was swinging with a sweet boy, and it was his turn to swing. I was pushing him, back and forth, this boy whose name I don't remember. Without warning, I pulled him back for another push and then I bit him. Hard.

I was a biter. Who knows why; maybe I was frustrated, or maybe I just wanted to say and do more than I was allowed. I was a biter for a few years, and all it got me was a string of day schools that kicked me out after yet another "episode" and a bunch of pissed-off teachers.

After biting this boy on the swing, I was swiftly escorted to the broom closet. It had a Dutch door; the top was open and the bottom was firmly shut. Snuggled between a mop pail and random bottles of cleaning supplies, I sat quietly in a little plastic chair, peering down the long hallway to the entrance as I waited for my dad.

In the light of the door, he appeared. He would save me. Take me home. Or maybe out for a root beer or a trip to the zoo. I saw him talking to the director. Their voices rose and they used some words that only grown-ups said. The director was having none of it. Their voices got louder.

"I had to take off work," he said. Then suddenly he stopped arguing and looked down the hall.

"What is my daughter doing in the broom closet?" he wanted to know. "You can't stick a kid in the broom closet; how long has she been there?"

He walked stiffly down the hall, reached over with his long daddy arms, and scooped me up over the door. I was safe. My dad gave the director a look.

The director said to take *all* of my things. And without warning, cuddled in my dad's arms, in front of the director, I bit my dad.

He took me outside where his 1970s baby blue VW Beetle sat in the street. Some of it was covered with gray spray paint. There weren't any seat belts, and if my mom was in the front, I rode in a plastic booster seat that I would slide onto the floorboard at stops. Some of the floorboards had rotten patches, and if I tilted my head at the right angle, I could see the road below.

He sat me down in the passenger seat and wrapped his arms around the steering wheel, laid his head down on the horn, and began to cry.

This was one of just two times I had ever seen my dad shed a tear.

"I am so sorry, Daddy. I will never, ever, ever do that again."

His shoulders continued to heave in the front seat.

"I promise I will never bite again. Please, please, stop crying."

My dad was weeping, head dropped. I pleaded and begged for him to stop.

I begged some more. He cried some more. I thought it would never end.

Without warning, his head popped up.

"Katrell," he said, suddenly somber and dry-eyed. "I didn't want to do this, but you have given me no choice. I wanted to wait until you were older, when you could understand better. I have a secret to tell you; it's a real secret that you can't ever tell anyone. Your life depends upon it; my life depends upon it. I have to tell you, but you have to promise me that no matter what, you will never, ever, ever tell a soul."

I was scared. But I wanted desperately to know what this important secret was and for him to please, please stop crying. I promised him, over and over, that I would never tell.

He pretended to really weigh this offer, sighed skeptically, and at last relented.

"You," he paused, then continued. "You have superpower teeth. And if you continue to waste your powers, when you really need them, they won't be there."

I never bit anyone again. And I believed this until I was fourteen.

※

I grew up poor. My parents had me when they were really just kids themselves. My parents met through friends, and one of their earliest dates was an Allman Brothers Band concert. For the better part of my youngest years, we lived in run-down government project housing. By the end of elementary school, I was a latchkey kid, making my way home every day, sometimes on foot and sometimes on the bus. I spent two hours alone every day until my parents came home. This is when I learned to bake. I would make concoctions that always included cups of sugar, sticks of butter, and Hershey's syrup. Sometimes I would add cinnamon or peanut butter or pancake syrup. This was stirred into a paste and spread on toasted bread to make sugar sandwiches.

After I finished my cooking, I would crank up my dad's record player with some Steve Miller Band and jump on the couch until I was tired enough to settle in for some exotic *Love Boat* reruns. Being a latchkey kid was totally acceptable then, especially in my neighborhood. I had no idea we were poor; I loved my collection of eclectic neighbors. The older Greek couple next door kept an eye on me. I enjoyed playing on the metal slide right outside our glass patio door; scalding in the hot sun, it always had pieces of melted diapers stuck to it in the summer months. You had to double up on pants to use it during the heat of the day, but that was good enough for me.

Tall and skinny, my dad paced the sidelines at all the sports events I participated in, like softball. I played right field, and when I got older, I graduated to shortstop. I was always oblivious and daydreaming, etching rainbows with puffy clouds in the red dirt with the toe of my cleats. Whenever the ball would roll my way I'd hear, "Look alive! Katrell! Please! Look alive!"

My poor dad. This was a common statement in my house. On the field at soccer or softball practice. At swimming lessons. Starting a new school or day camp. (But never, ever at the skating rink.)

I played a lot of sports. I was pretty much thrown into everything, as long as it cost less than seventy dollars a season, you didn't have to try out, and you could walk away with one generic jersey. It was a plus if they encouraged beer for the parents.

I was average at best.

Yet my dad was my own personal coach, complete with pep talks on the way to games or meets. We'd play basketball before dinner or toss the softball around the yard. He taught me how to swim by busting a roll of quarters on the side of the pool. He'd toss them in and, say, "You get 'em, you keep 'em." This was one of his "motivational fabrications," as I liked to call them.

This was my dad's idea of keeping me involved and, as an only child, that was important. I had to work for friends. Be funny. Don't sass. Always smile. Use good manners. Practice teamwork. It was a constant balancing act to stay in the good graces of the other girls who had a built-in brood of sisters and brothers.

A lot of only children fall into two categories with their parents—the princess or the friend. I was definitely the friend. I was hauled along to adult cookouts, ball games, and neighborhood parties. I'd bring my art supplies and, once I scoped out the desserts, I'd settle into a corner or couch to sketch my masterpieces of dogs or kittens falling out of baskets. Sometimes my parents and their hippie friends would call on me to do my Louis Armstrong impression by singing "Hello Dolly" in the back of my throat to their hysterical laughter and applause.

They would take me along on rambling road trips to see outdoor craft and music festivals around the South. Bluegrass. Jazz. Rock. It didn't matter. I'd curl up on the corduroy bed in the back of our Chevy van in my sundress and nibble the pieces off a candy necklace.

My dad was always on my side. He taught me to give and never give up.

When I was little and someone would bend down and coo, "Ooh, isn't she just the cutest thing?" he would reply, "She might be cute but she's smart as a whip, and she's gonna do great things."

With my dad, the sky was always the limit. And I was never hindered by a poufy dress with a giant bow or told to stay away from mud puddles. In fact, he once threatened to send me to an Outward Bound camp—a three-month wilderness retreat—because I spent my babysitting money on a hair crimper.

One day, he and I went to Daytona Beach. We collected all the colorful shells we could find, put them in holes that we had dug in the sand, and let blocks of wax melt around them in the hot sun to make candles. That was my dad's favorite day.

While I enjoyed an idyllic, albeit not glamorous, childhood, Midtown Atlanta, where I grew up, was hit or miss. It was the South, and race colored everything. It could be confusing for a kid, but I took my example from my grandfather, Lieutenant Colonel Ren Christie. A drill instructor on Parris Island who fought in both World War II and the Korean War, he would later go on to be a drama teacher. He was a big softie but demanded respect at the same time.

My grandfather spent twenty-four years in the marines. When he returned home, he finished earning his degrees at the University of Georgia and became head of the speech and drama department at Valdosta State University.

Ren was the kind of guy who had his hands in everything. He taught Dale Carnegie courses in public speaking. He was heavy into the Rotary Club, was a Sunday school teacher, and always wore a fedora and rode a bicycle everywhere. Everyone called him Dr. Christie.

What he loved the most was the Valdosta Wildcats high school football team. In the 1980s, the Wildcats were in the process of becoming the winningest high school team in the country. Many of the kids on the team were underprivileged and had been bused in from surrounding black communities. He decided the best way he could help was to make sure the athletes got a solid, hot meal the night before the games. So he lined up the Valdosta football fanatic fans (most of whom were white) to offer homemade meals for the players (largely black) in their homes. In his own small way, he showed me that color lines were meaningless and little things can make a big change in someone's life—and also that you lead with actions and not just words. He offered a scholarship at Valdosta State because he believed that education was the ladder up.

Ren died at age eighty-four, and he made a voice recording for his family so he could narrate his own funeral service. It was weird, but it was also completely him. We listened to him thank us all for coming and tell us what a terrific life he'd had. He gave us one last pep talk for life, and then they played "Taps."

Thanks to my grandfather's generosity, I was forced to attend a fancy private school in Atlanta for a few years. I was totally out of my league. It was the kind of place where one of my best friends was picked up and dropped off in a baby blue Rolls Royce. My dad would pull up in his big, orange, state-issued, Department of Transportation pickup truck. For a while, this was really cool. The other kids wanted to play with the light on top of the cab. They would motion for him to honk the horn.

But suddenly one day, about the time I reached middle school, it wasn't so cool anymore. Instead, it dawned on me that I was the broke kid with the dad in the Day-Glo truck owned by the state. It was strange to look around and suddenly realize that I was in a completely different social stratosphere than my classmates. It hadn't occurred to me before then that they had so much more money than I had and what that meant.

Designer jeans were all the rage when I was in school. But we shopped at secondhand stores, so I was at the mercy of whatever hand-me-downs were available on any particular day. I remember being thrilled to discover a pair of Jordache jeans. They were a little scuffed up, but still the right brand with bright pink stitching. My mom made the purchase, and I was beyond excited to wear them to school for the first time.

I got looks alright. One of the popular girls sashayed over to me in the hall and told me matter-of-factly that my superawesome Jordache jeans had once been hers. That fluorescent pink stitching I was so proud of? It was a dead giveaway. She'd donated them after getting a nicer new pair. Ask any middle school girl who has worn the wrong brand of jeans how important that can be.

Thankfully, my family showed me that loads of money don't always buy happiness, bright pink stitching or not. In fact, our best memories were made with pennies.

We had a tradition in our family that on your birthday, it was your day and you could choose whatever you wanted to do. Everyone had to go along with it, no complaints. One year, on the morning of my dad's birthday, he came down to Atlanta from my parents' house in the 'burbs. I was living in my first big-girl apartment on a very busy street. My apartment was the corner unit on the bottom floor. I claimed the small patch of grass with a few mismatched flowerpots that rounded the corner where two sidewalks met.

My dad's birthday wish: that we buy two really fat Cuban knock-off cigars, a small plastic kiddie pool, and all the Grand Funk Railroad albums we could find at the Wax and Facts record store. We hauled my stereo, my two floor speakers (which doubled as my cats' scratching pad), and a record player out into my yard.

My dad hauled two very frayed green and white plastic and aluminum lawn chairs from the trunk of his car. We sat outside all day in the sun on the busy road and drank our beer—feet in the kiddie pool—blasting all our new Grand Funk Railroad albums and smoking our cigars.

My favorite day.

Chapter 5

HE CARRIED A TIFFANY'S BAG

"My friends are my estate;
forgive me then the avarice
to hoard them."

—Emily Dickinson

 y Southern upbringing was full of an eccentric cast of characters. Like Don . . . or Dawn. It was your choice. He introduced himself both ways. Whatever made you most uncomfortable. When I was born, his longtime friend lived near my parents, so I grew up with him always in my periphery.

He is forty-three years and one day older than me. But mentally, we were both in the same place. Whenever I'd ask him the age of someone we were discussing, he'd always reply, "Oh, you know, our age."

He never wore the same shirt twice. And every Friday for twenty-six years, he ate dinner with his best friend. They never used the same flatware. It was a tradition. Every week, they'd scour thrift stores for a new place setting, and every week, they'd donate the last one used.

We became friends. Good friends. As good as a gay sixty-year-old man and a scattered straight young teenage girl could be. It was perfection. He was the Laverne to my Shirley. He thought I was the Eliza to his Professor Henry Higgins.

He asked me to dinner one night and we started our own tradition: the same place, the same time, every week. We'd meet up in the same high-backed, red, shiny booth. He always ordered the same thing, a T-bone steak with cottage cheese, which he spread on top. All the staff loved him—his weekly show and generous tips. The waitresses buzzed around in their white hats that looked like dinner napkins. He liked to sit in the middle of the restaurant on display.

Every week, he'd gleefully reach under the table and pull out a somewhat tattered shopping bag in the telltale robin's egg blue with TIFFANY's etched across the front. He waved it around like a flag to draw as much attention as possible and then sent me into the bathroom to change.

It was always a surprise. A vintage outfit or costume. Sometimes good, sometimes bad. Sometimes beyond bad. But it made him happy, and we were friends.

These outfits included but were not limited to:

- Jackie O suits
- 1970s onesie ice-skating costumes
- Sequined majorette uniforms
- Vintage Genie
- Capes
- Anything resembling drag

- *Designing Women* shoulder-pad power suits
- Full-length ballroom gowns
- Over-the-top quinceañera dresses
- Anything pink
- Everything bedazzled, glittery, and ruffled

I'd wedge myself into whatever ridiculousness he'd brought along and promenade back to the booth. He'd ask for a couple of twirls and then declare that I looked "mahvelooous."

I would say, "I love it," no matter what, and he'd stick out his hand with his giant diamond pinky ring and twirl me into my seat while all the other old queens in the place gawked.

Our monthly outings included, but were not limited to, art house films, antiquing, thrifting, pretentious dinners with his Chihuahua Dot, returning things, touring around his yard to admire his garden, and organizing his porn and classic movie collections.

We visited the dive bars in Atlanta he hadn't been kicked out of, as well as the ones he had, pretending he was his twin brother (Don has an identical twin and they lived together). He introduced me as his daughter and, if given a look, resorted to granddaughter.

We hit all the Salvation Army and Nearly New shops, where he loved to purchase horribly tacky or completely crappy items and give them to people, saying, "I saw this and I immediately thought of you."

We watched and talked about *Madam Butterfly* and listened to opera blaring in his car. He spent a lot of time reminiscing about his hometown, Chicago.

His mother was a cleaning lady at Tiffany's & Co. (the stained glass, not the jewelry). Whether this was true or not, I don't know, but it was the gospel according to Don. Every year, as a holiday gift, some of the staff would receive a lamp made from the scraps of the windows that were commissioned. Don's mother saved the lamps year after year, and when she retired, she gave them to her two boys. As adults, they sold off a few to start their empire in the gold and gilded, flora and fauna, Liberace-inspired antique shop where they held court.

Like Statler and Waldorf from the Muppets, these two unruly queens hurled harsh and sometimes humorous suggestions at the customers from behind the front counter. If you looked upset, they'd immediately turn you on to a new vintage fainting couch, marked down, of course, or something they said was owned by Bette Davis's assistant.

Their tiny shop was wedged between a Jack Shack and Tattletails strip club on Piedmont Avenue in Atlanta. A big pink Cadillac with the shop name painted on the side sits outside. It was a land-mark for a while.

Once we were invited to a mutual friend's wedding at a fancy country club. Don picked me up in the minivan he used to shuffle his priceless, one-of-a-kind, rare finds back and forth. It had at least ten wrecked places on it where he'd backed over a curb after deciding he "just couldn't handle the traffic anymore" and needed to make an emergency U-turn.

When we arrived at the wedding, he sauntered up to the front row, waving his blue Tiffany's bag over his head. He smacked every-one in the face with it as he shimmied down the aisle to sit down.

As one of the ushers milled about, nowhere near us, Don cupped his hand around his mouth and said in a loud, raspy whisper-scream, "Here's my gift, make sure it gets to the gift table. You know it came from Tiiiiffaaaanny's!!!!!!!"

A few weeks later, I ran into the bride and asked her what was in the bag. She rolled her eyes and shook her head in disgust.

"You don't want to know," she said. "It's just Don being tacky."

Once he gave my boss a two-foot-tall Carrera marble penis statue at my company Christmas party.

After a couple of weeks of prodding, the bride finally told me. It was a silver wedding knife—the type that comes in a long, shallow, slender box with the viewable window on top—with a lacy boutonniere tied to the handle. *Not bad*, I thought—until she told me that it had another couple's names and wedding date inscribed on the blade.

Don taught me a lot of things: how to sit like a lady, not to mix vintage jewelry styles, and always send thank-you cards. But two things really stand out. One is that you shouldn't give a shit what people think. The other is that family doesn't always mean blood relative. Sometimes the family you find can be just as important to you as the family you were born into. Don was a one-of-a-kind find, and he was family.

Chapter 6

THE DIRTY SOUTH

> "I don't want to die without
> any scars."
>
> —Chuck Palahniuk, *Fight Club*

 rowing up, all the cool kids hung out at the local skating rink. This might have been because they sold beer to dads and played nonstop sports on a giant TV balanced on a broken rolling cart in the concession area.

Many dads became a lot less worried about broken bones or falls after a couple of beers.

That skating rink concession area might have been the original man cave. All the basics were covered: beer, sports, neon-lit metal posters, a few video games and pinball, pizza, nachos, and a Slurpee machine.

No one was nagging you to get your shoes off the seat or to steer clear of the decorative throw pillows. You could stick your gum under the table and it was pretty much expected that you peed on the bathroom walls. A DJ was at your beck and call with a whole bunch of loud metal music and a few slow jams thrown in for variety.

Every tenth time I'd circle the rink, my dad would throw up a hand to let me think he was watching. Then the Braves nailed a home run and the dad zone erupted in cheers. Skate sessions usually started and ended around game times.

My love for skating never wavered. You can work out a lot of your sixth-grade issues listening to Pat Benatar while skating backward and doing your hair with a vent brush. I had my first kiss at the roller rink.

I joined in the hokey pokey and sometimes the chariot races. But I'd usually skate off and hide in the bathroom during couples skate. This was when the dads would abandon the TVs and come lean against the carpet wall. They'd throw on their best macho, arms-crossed stance while they watched their daughters skate around, holding hands with some too-cool-for-school boy. As soon as it was over, they would go back to yelling at the TV.

I'd hop into the car afterward, sweaty and smelling of cigarettes. I'd peel off my soaked socks and silently tally up my number of falls. Falling down in front of other kids—maybe even the school crush—was devastating. No one else really cared, of course. But it was something I might go over in my head a couple of million times before asking to sit down at the popular lunch table.

But most of my angst about jeans or jerky school kids could usually be skated out in the rink. A few laps to Chaka Khan and my focus would shift from the bullies to balancing. More than ten falls was not a good skate day. Fewer than five falls was okay. Sometimes I would blame my wipeouts on the little kids who got in my way. Sometimes it was my wheels. Other times it was gum or puke on the rink.

As I got older, I realized that the slower you skate, the less you fall down. The fewer chances you take, the better off you are. It became easier to just play it safe and look cool and stop trying to get better or try to learn new tricks. There were a few perfect days in my elementary and middle school years where there were no falls at all.

Years later, when I tried out for Roller Derby, I did it with a group of women I'd been friends with for a couple of years. I knew almost nothing about the game except that you got to wear something wild and skate. I still had balance. I could skate backward. And I liked loud music. I was also yearning for exercise and to get out of the hot kitchen at my tea shop. It helped that practice was at the same rink where I'd grown up skating.

My team was the Toxic Shocks in the Dirty South Derby league. I adopted the name Takillya Sunrise, which had already been my nickname for years (you can guess the reason). I would skate out wearing one crazy costume or another with my face painted up like a drag queen voodoo doll. I had huge hair and a tool belt slung on my waist stocked with tequila shooters and tampons. It was a blast. Some of my best friends today came from those five years of playing derby.

Every neighborhood and personality type was represented on that team. And it wasn't what you might expect. There were lawyers, an archaeologist, and an epidemiologist with the Centers for Disease Control.

If you've ever seen a Roller Derby bout, what you probably remember is the players all skating really fast around the track and nailing each other. When you're out there, it's extremely physical and really loud. There is hard rock music blaring. I came out of bouts bruised and sore.

I learned a lot as I played. I learned it's occasionally fun to knock someone's block off. I learned that big thighs are deadly, especially when they have a giant Virgin Mary tattooed on them. I learned that women of every size should be proud because Roller Derby needs power, and this comes in big, strong packages. In derby, girls would sometimes put on extra pounds before game day.

But what really clicked for me was the business and party side of the whole thing. I was head of events and planned some truly epic after parties. I won the "Closing Time Award" more than once. I may not have been the strongest player, but I was great at chatting up the league and getting people to show up at the games.

I also discovered that some fans came to Roller Derby bouts because they wanted to see gals skating around in their underwear. My committee started selling advertisements on "bout panties"— the granny panties that we'd wear for matches, and we learned that certain advertisers wanted their names on certain butts, sort of like NASCAR.

I admit, this may not have been the most progressive, feminist thing to do, but it raised a ton of money for a league struggling to get their first rink. One season we raked in almost $10,000 in bout panty ads. That was definitely a bigger contribution to the league than my mediocre blocking.

The things I can say about my Roller Derby career:

- I was not the best skater, but I don't think I was the worst. I could be wrong.

- Skating around in a circle in a fun outfit to a kick-ass song was my talent.
- Skating around in a circle and pummeling people was not.

I joined Roller Derby for the costumes, the camaraderie, the exercise, and the fun.

Over time, Roller Derby has changed. The biggest change is that it has become a serious sport. Tutus have been traded for gym shorts, and tequila shots before the games have been replaced with squats. When I played, at least for me, it was pure, unorganized campiness: WWF wrestling with a little *Rocky Horror Picture Show* thrown in—and a whole bunch of fun.

Back when I started in Roller Derby, on that first day of practice in Atlanta, our coach gathered us in a circle in the middle of the rink. She explained that it didn't matter if we weren't the best skaters, hadn't practiced in years, or didn't know all the rules. They would work with us, she said. She talked about dedication, being a team player, hard work, and giving 100 percent.

But she said the most important thing you need to learn in derby—the thing that will determine your success or failure in the sport—is your ability to fall and recover, to get back up and keep going.

Chapter 7

WHERE THE MOUNTAINS MEET THE MIST

"Darkness cannot drive out darkness,
only light can do that.
Hate cannot drive out hate,
only love can do that."

—Dr. Martin Luther King Jr.

fter my failed attempt at gardening in Hyderabad, Cate's handicraft project goes ahead of schedule. I decide to use the extra time to visit Darjeeling, where my tea comes from. Darjeeling is an isolated hill station in the northeastern reaches of India, tucked in along the borders of China, Tibet, Bhutan, and Nepal in the Himalayan Mountains. Buddhists once controlled the area, and then the Nepalese, before the British seized the territory in the nineteenth century.

The British and Scottish originally settled Darjeeling as a sanatorium to escape the hot Indian climate. Seeing that the cool, misty mountain climate was ideal for growing tea, they imported seeds from nearby China. Tea plantations sprang up and remain the region's main resource.

Known as the Queen of the Hills, Darjeeling is nestled into the mountainside so that everything is vertical. Anywhere you go, you're going to be walking up or down a hill, usually on a steep switchback. You want buns of steel? Wander around Darjeeling for a few days.

The airport closest to Darjeeling is Bagdogra, a military base at the foot of the mountains. I arrive and book a prepaid taxi. A taxi here is a 4×4 because that's what will make it up the narrow, rutted road.

As I exit the airport, everyone is yelling at me, sizing me up. With a fixed price, they want to see who might be willing to settle for a luxury 4×4 without the luxury. They are looking for who might tip, who might need too many bathroom breaks, or who will want to stop to take loads of photos. They also want to see if you look green enough so you wouldn't object if they stop to pick up other travelers or friends for extra cash on the way.

But at the time I don't know any of this. I simply hop into my gigantic Land Cruiser, and my driver throws my luggage onto the top rack.

The trek is one of the most intense and beautiful six hours of my life. First we drive for an hour through rolling tea fields. Women are picking tea leaves in bright dresses, straw baskets on their backs. Next we move through small villages with roadside tea huts and hot samosas hanging over pots of bubbling oil. Cows, goats, and pigs meander leisurely back and forth across the road.

The journey becomes more mountainous as we begin passing elephant crossing signs. The vegetation morphs from tropical plants to twisted banyan trees, bamboo, and pointed firs that reach into the mist. The weather gets steadily colder, and I have the driver stop so I can get into my luggage on the roof and pull on a coat and boots.

The road is carved out of the sides of the mountains. It's unpaved, made of tiny sandy pebbles. At some points it's washed out completely, with boards jammed between the drops. We swoop into what looks like a storm cloud, which I could see from the airport. It's wet and it drenches my clothes through the windows. I can't see five feet in front of the Land Cruiser. Houses and whole towns emerge from the mist without warning. At certain points I just close my eyes and breathe. The stillness is broken by the sounds of horns as drivers alert each other that they are coming around the slender hairpin turns, slowly climbing this mountain.

Finally, we pass through the clouds and are met with a crash of sunlight. It's an entirely new world. The sky opens up. Jutting cliffs with tiny buildings teeter on ridges. I can see the fog rolling down the snowcapped mountains.

About midway to the top, we stop for hot tea and *momos*, which are small, steamed dumplings that are served at a wooden building secured to the mountain by stilts. A chubby stray dog wanders over to say hello and sniff out the foreigner.

At the end of the road, the Land Cruiser lurches to a stop. The driver throws some rocks underneath the wheels and hauls my luggage down from the roof. He points uphill on a one-lane street toward the town.

I settle into a cozy, wooden hotel room complete with a cat and an oil heater. There are a lot of windows, each one with a lock to keep out the nosy monkeys hanging out on the roof. The blanket on the bed is as heavy as five rugs. Two little straw chairs sit against the window. They look out and down to the tiered city teetering on the side of the mountain above the clouds.

During this whole trip, an idea had slowly been brewing. At this point, all I know is that I want it to involve Dr. Bombay's, my community, and tea. Beyond that, the details are murky. Maybe I can help by donating books or paying for someone's school fees.

I had e-mailed and called countless people, but everything is at a dead end. So I arrive on a Monday night with no plan.

The next morning I am at an Internet café posting pictures when a huge group of people forms a human chain around the center of town as part of a political protest. There's been unrest in the area. My trip up here was delayed because of sometimes violent protests. Turns out, the Gorkhas aren't so happy about having this region taken away all those years ago. Subversive Gorkhaland signs are everywhere around the city.

I'm locked in the breakfast place for two hours until the rally ends. With time to kill, I talk to the guy who runs the shop and tell him what I am trying to do. He suggests I try a fair-trade women's co-op store. His suggestion sets off a chain of events that has me hiking up all those hills I mentioned:

- the co-op sends me to a fair-trade tea representative,
- who directs me to a women's center,
- that sends me (mistakenly) to an insane asylum,
- which leads to another fair-trade tea company.
- The Angels of Charity is next,
- then to a mammogram clinic,

- then comes a privately owned chai tea project,
- then a Hindu girls' school,
- there are a few more stops along the way,
- before I wind up at the massive metal door of a Buddhist orphanage.

The orphanage holds about forty-five girls between the ages of three and seventeen. It's way too crowded. Some of the girls are lucky enough to have bunk beds, but the rest sleep in a loft area on pads.

Although he doesn't live there, the monk who is in charge makes the girls keep everything neat and tidy. The walls are painted in bright colors. There is one common room they use for studying, eating, and praying.

One thing hits me right away. When the girls turn seventeen, they're on their own. There isn't funding for them to continue after that point. For the girls who leave, this can lead to being in the sex trade, living on the streets, or doing manual labor for the rest of their lives. Some simply go missing.

Five of the girls are nearing graduation, and I quickly figure that this is where I should be. I take pictures of them, mug-shot style, and write their names on a chalkboard behind them so I can learn them. The teachers and housekeepers jump in at the end of the line because, not speaking any English, they have no idea what I'm doing. They run and put on their best clothes and do their makeup before this glamour shot. They are giggling and excited.

After the first day at the orphanage, the girls start calling me "sister." I go shopping and buy them art supplies, and they all make me cards, each one addressed "To Sister Katrell."

Awww, that's so sweet! I'm like their big sister, I think.

I'm the cool big sister who breezes in with tacky fingernail polish, big hair, loud music, and bad American trendy mall clothes.

About the third night, I find out they thought I was a nun.

Little do they know that for the last three-plus years, Sister Katrell has been skating around in a circle in her underwear, chain-smoking and publicly drinking booze from the bottle.

I spend every night at the orphanage hanging with the girls. We fill hours drawing Minnie and Mickey Mouse in the Himalayan Mountains. Their orphanage has a couple of books. One is a tattered little Disney hardback, something you would pick up at Big Lots in the dollar bin. They are constantly engrossed in it. They treat it like gold.

The time I spend at this orphanage is pretty magical. Lots of drawing and hair braiding. I bring fruit and they feed me rice and dal. They have a lovely cat that sleeps in a little padded box outside the kitchen. I try to help them with their schoolwork. We take long walks around the town and they do their best to piece together English words describing the tea.

They try to teach me songs in Nepali. Amazingly enough, they know one English song: "We Shall Overcome." Another local woman who comes in to help fills in the gaps on their backgrounds. Jampa, the monk, outlines the desperation.

I listen, but I am already in—hook, line, and sinker. I'm taking mental notes of the needs. The oldest girls are the most at risk. Three of them are set to turn seventeen and will have to leave within a year. So they become my crew. We quickly become inseparable.

Manoj was born into a middle-class family with multiple sons who still live in the town. They gave her up to the orphanage when she was little because they just didn't want a girl.

Labuki has also been at the orphanage since she was a small toddler. Her mom was mostly homeless and worked for pennies as a day laborer, breaking stones in the riverbed to make concrete.

Devna has no living parents, although she did have an uncle that lived eight hours away by train.

One night I take them to a restaurant. It isn't a fancy place but it isn't street food either. The four of us sit down, and when the waiter appears at our table and hands us menus, the girls look scared and confused.

We silently study the list of food. When I ask what they are going to order, they say they don't know.

"Get anything you want," I say encouragingly.

This is followed by a few minutes of oohing and aahing—but no progress.

I figure they might be overwhelmed by the choices.

"Maybe we can just get a bunch of dishes and share," I suggest.

"Share what?" they ask.

"Share the food. Whatever we order," I explain.

It becomes clear to me that they don't understand. They have never been inside a restaurant. Sure, they'd walked by them on the street. But they had no idea what was going on inside. They are shocked to learn that all of these food items on the menu are just sitting there in the kitchen at that very moment waiting to be cooked, plated, and whisked out to our table. When the waiter brings our dinner, they thank him at least a thousand times.

The same thing happens when we take a taxi to a nearby tea plantation. They scream and giggle when the driver cranks the ignition. They have never even sat in a car before.

I soon learn there have been many "nevers" in their lives.

They have never had a shower. All bathing is done with a cold bucket of water, if water is even available. They have never had someone really cut their hair. That was done with a dull knife at the orphanage. Little things we do every day are brand-new experiences for them. Unlike me, they never had a dad to lace up their skates. They have never been given the ability to dream.

One night we have a conversation about their futures. What do they hope to be when they grow up? What kind of jobs do they want? Do they want to get married or be a mom one day?

They don't have answers. The fear that consumes them is leaving the orphanage. This is the furthest they can think. What will happen on the day that they are asked to gather their things and leave? To walk out the door and be all alone, standing on the street with no one to turn to and nowhere to go?

When I first arrived, all three girls lied to me about their age, hoping to avoid the unavoidable. They were hoping no one noticed they were growing up.

On my walk back to my hotel, I start weighing it all. I begin thinking of things I can hawk when I return home. My struggling tea shop is barely paying the bills. I haven't seen a paycheck in months. I'd begged my boyfriend to hold down the fort and paid someone to work my shifts at the tea shop while I was gone.

But I just can't walk away. I'll figure out some way—if I have to fight tooth and nail—to come back here and make this right.

Whatever I do would barely scrape the surface.

But is something better than nothing? I wonder. The oppression is mind-boggling.

I've always wondered about the South. How could people who thought of themselves as good, who went to church on Sundays and supposedly followed their Ten Commandments, how had they talked about or acted when they encountered slavery? I always imagined either someone horsewhipping a slave or the country grandma who builds a relationship with one of her servants.

It's the in between that I have never been able to imagine, until now. It means eating with people starving or dying outside the restaurant window. It's walking down the street with your kid while you're stepping over an old, crippled woman on her deathbed, shaking a can. It's the person who lives under the stairs and only comes out with a tray of tea when called upon. It's the four-year-olds who rush onto a train at the stops on their hands and knees to wipe down people's shoes for a penny.

And then it's the upper caste, who don't even seem to notice this is going on and can keep the cricket conversation going in a taxi with little kids banging on the window for food. It's like two completely different worlds, living in the same space, mere inches from each other. I had thought about this many times over my life, about the in between.

But now these three girls are burned into my mind. They are real. They have feelings. They aren't just an article about poverty or a picture on Facebook. They are living here on the other side of the world, in a tiny town in the middle of nowhere, with no one to turn to. All they need are basic necessities: a roof over their heads, food, and the ability to continue going to school. These are things I can provide.

During my final days in Darjeeling, I spend all my time with them. I take photos of us together and have them printed out at the local computer store. I write my name and address in big letters on each one and hang them on the wall above their mats.

But realistically, there is no way for them to contact me. I say my good-byes and tell them to give me six months. I'll be back. Then they wave and close the big metal doors and I hear the lock catch. I'm on the street alone, and I promise I will never be the in between.

Chapter 8

DR. BOMBAY'S UNDERWATER TEA PARTY

> "Choose a job you love and you will never have to work a day in your life."
>
> —Confucius

 can still hear the clang of the orphanage's steel door in Darjeeling when I touch down again in Atlanta. I am home, but nothing is the same. I'm back at my tea shop, up to my elbows in dough or working the counter. But my mind is in the mountains half a world away. I wrack my brain to come up with a way to help the girls and decide I will sell Darjeeling tea and use the profits toward scholarships for the girls. Through help from my friends on Facebook, we come up with a name for the project—the Learning Tea.

I dig up a glass fishbowl collecting dust in my storage closet and handwrite a note explaining where I'd been and what I'd seen. I ask my customers to drop in any extra change and I promise to take their donations back to Darjeeling and do what I can with the money they give. I open a savings account, and every Monday I deposit the change I collect from the people who I've come to know as friends since opening this place.

My tea shop. How that came to be deserves a little explanation.

I've always collected things. Some people call it junk. I call them amazing treasures.

Little odds and ends. Vintage furniture that no one would buy. Box lots that no one bid on. Some red velvet stage curtains that came out of an opera theater in Paris. A lime green chaise that wouldn't sell because the springs were busted. Old Asian parasols. Tons of weathered, oddly framed photographs. More books than you could shake a stick at. Some gold vinyl stools from the 1970s. And that's just naming a few. I carefully carted my treasures from one apartment to the next, collecting a little more with each move.

My parents came over one day for lunch and told me that things were getting ridiculous. My one-bedroom apartment was, as my mom put it, "full up."

"Katrell, seriously, you need more space or you've got to get rid of some things."

I'm not one of those hoarders you see on reality TV shows. My things were tidy, neatly arranged, and very well kept. But I do love a discount.

All my years of friendship with Don taught me to appreciate vintage items. Some of my stuff came from him. Other finds were from flea markets or local yard sales. Still others I'd pick up off the side of the road. Don and I would sit around and make up grand tales about the lineage of some rhinestone brooch or beat-up ottoman.

I've always loved art. For years I worked at an auction house/ antique store. It was a huge building with rare one-of-a-kind treasures that would be snapped up for hundreds of thousands of dollars. Celebrities would peruse our quarterly catalogs and send in big checks or dispatch their assistants to bid on things like vintage cars or twenty-foot, hand-carved mantels that had been hauled out of some old castle in Europe.

Most of the time, I repaired paintings in a musty basement. But between art jobs, I would venture upstairs to plan events or fill in as my boss's personal assistant. My boss was an eccentric and savvy businessman. He had a taste for the elite and the odd.

He didn't care how something got done, as long as the finished product met his expectations and it was done yesterday. I learned a lot from him and his rules. You used whatever resources you had, and if you didn't have any, you'd better find some. Network. Get on the phone. Go out. Meet people. You are only as capable as you think you are.

He did everything in life with the utmost extravagance, from ordering real Chicago pizza that he Fed-Exed in for his lunch to hiring Kool and the Gang to play his disco-themed auction parties. He would send me off on some seemingly impossible tasks, fully expecting they would get done. There really wasn't any other choice.

This job gave me some great opportunities to harness my inner badass. He expected nothing less. I was able to meet some legends in the art world, and I even spent a year as a buyer in Italy for one of his customers who was opening a gallery. I also restored paintings on the side for a few choice clients at my apartment. It was a lonely job, as I usually worked by myself.

At this point I lived in Candler Park, one of Atlanta's older in-town neighborhoods, named after the founder of Coca-Cola.

Nowadays, it's home to quite a few Volvos and jogging strollers. But back then, it was sort of hip and scruffy.

In the small strip of business along the main drag of McLendon Avenue, there was a little ice-cream shop. They had a thirty-tub ice-cream cooler, an espresso machine, and not a single chair in the place. The walls were painted drab gray and there was one chalkboard on the wall with the drink list. This shop kept me going. An espresso for breakfast, another one at lunch, and then, if it was a long night, maybe a double.

One day as I stopped in for my caffeine fix, the manager told me the place was up for sale. The owner had a bigger place across town and said she just couldn't split her time between the two.

I thought about my espresso addiction. I thought about making my own sad little coffee alone at home. And then I would go back to thinking of the shop.

"There's an interested buyer," the manager told me one day when I popped in.

Gosh, I thought, *I love this place*. It was sterile, not a lot of personality. But I loved the idea of a little neighborhood hangout.

Each time I'd walk in I would ask, "How long do we have?"

I was obsessed with how much time remained before my work fuel was going to disappear and I would have to get in my car to drive for a fix.

As I was leaving, she yelled after me, "Thanks, have a good day."

And then, almost as an afterthought, she added, "If you bought it, you could have all the coffee you wanted."

Fucking funny, I thought. Me running a coffee shop? I can't even remember to return movies on time. It was a long walk home that

day. The idea of saying good-bye to our little neighborhood estab-
lishment depressed me. And, as I walked, I thought of all the great
things about that place. How all the kids rode their bikes there after
school. How the neighbors stopped to chat on the way to work.
How it was the reward for birthdays or straight As or game-day
celebrations. I thought about the friendly staff and how clean the
place looked. The hours didn't seem that long.

Then I started thinking of things that might go in there next,
this cool, old building with the beautiful double French doors. A
check-cashing place? A bail bonds office? An ammo shop? A weird
insurance company with metal blinds drawn tight? I thought about
the history of that place and how it had beautiful high ceilings and
a jiggly gold doorknob with a vintage mail slot in the door. And
then I thought about my treasures.

I went directly home, called the bank, and began to beg for
money.

No, I didn't have restaurant experience. I did have Mr. Coffee
coffeemaker experience. And I did spend a lot of summers and
holidays with my grandma baking things to fill up the lazy Susan.

The shop's owner was totally on board. She told me she would
give me sixty hours of training if I bought it so I snapped it up for
pennies. Within a week my friends showed up to paint and help
fill the little place with my life's collection of exotic, rare finds. I
knew once the neighborhood saw my array of dilapidated crap,
wild horses couldn't keep them away.

Maybe it wasn't the smartest decision I've ever made. Mone-
tarily, it was probably the worst. But if happiness were money, I'd
be a millionaire.

I can't say it's been easy. Often it's been really, really hard. The business is constantly struggling to stay afloat. But hard doesn't always mean unhappy, and sometimes busting your ass for something you believe in feels wonderful.

I've had some truly amazing employees. And I could write a whole book on the incredibly bad ones. I have heard some awful lies and legendary excuses, like the time one twenty-something told me she needed a single day off because her mother had died and then showed up the next day tan and smiling, a kayak strapped to the roof of her car.

When you're a small business owner with a part-time staff, someone not showing up means you do. I've missed weddings and birthdays and funerals. I didn't take a vacation for the first six years. I pretty much lived there. I'm not complaining. Before I jumped in feet first, I probably should've considered that I wasn't exactly going to get rich when the highest-priced single item on the menu was three dollars. And creating a warm, cozy environment that people don't want to leave doesn't translate into them spending lots of money.

But I feel like I hit my mark, creating a space the community could call their own, reading, playing the piano, laughing, and celebrating life. While Dr. Bombay's is not a big moneymaker, I do know 90 percent of my customers by name. I get to see the kids in the neighborhood grow up. I'm always invited to birthday parties, mainly because I'm working them. And I'm able to rally the neighborhood for causes I believe in.

The paint was still drying on the walls the day I officially opened the store. I went to Target and bought a small bookshelf. I wrote a note and taped it to the shelf. It said, "Drop off your old books. I will sell them for $1 and give the money to the local elementary school library." We sell the books, but anyone can also come in and sit and read them whenever they want. Within a couple of years, we raised the money for the school library to purchase more than one thousand books. We also donated to a circus animal rescue farm and Katrina victims.

My business partner and then-boyfriend Nick is the unsung hero of all this. We started out as best friends. For years we hung out, went to see shows, and used each other as sounding boards for bad relationship drama.

At one point we found ourselves both running from crappy relationships at the same time and ended up making a go of it. It didn't take us very long to realize that while we enjoyed jumping on the bed drunk, staying up until dawn making peanut butter pancakes, and watching Freedom Rock commercials, we didn't fit as a couple. We've both moved far away from being lovers but have an enormous amount of love and compassion for the shop and the project.

We served coffee and tea. But Nick is British and he brought a real flair to the tea side of the shop that the customers seemed to prefer, so we became a tea shop.

If you're ever in the neighborhood and drop by, he'll make you the perfect cup of PG Tips and throw in a scone from his mother's recipe book. He'll be the guy behind the counter who sounds like a pirate from Wilshire, England, wearing a pair of chucks and a Metallica T-shirt.

It's been ten years since we opened the shop. We've taken over the space next door. On weekends we're often filled up with bridal showers or kids' birthday parties. The teapots are flea market finds. Nothing matches. And I am proud to say my little bookshelf has multiplied. Dr. Bombay's is filled with treasures, sticky kids' handprints on record players, raunchy teenage bathroom graffiti, an upright piano that "can be played if you can," and home to more than ten thousand books that all cost a dollar.

And, just as the book collection multiplied, slowly the money in the fishbowl accumulated as my customers sipped their coffee and hot chai, a new recipe I'd procured from my travels. After six months, my little shop had collected $4,000 from people just standing at the counter reading my note and listening to my endless stories about the girls and Darjeeling. My own awesome community had responded.

Saving up my own tips to cover my travel arrangements, I counted down the days until I could see the girls again.

Chapter 9

THE RETURN TO INDIA

"Do. Or do not. There is no try."

—Yoda

 he first order of business was to apply for another visa because mine had only been valid for six months. I never thought I'd actually *want* to go back. This time, I pack even lighter but bring along a pair of sturdy boots and a big, warm coat. I make arrangements with my favorite hotel in Darjeeling, and in the spring, just as the dogwoods are beginning to bloom in Atlanta, I am off again to make good on the promise I made the girls.

After a thirty-one-hour flight with two layovers followed by a restless night in Mumbai, I arrive back in Darjeeling around two in the afternoon, exhausted but high on adrenaline. I am really doing this. I throw down my bags, grab a quick shower, and book it back to the orphanage.

All of those days back in Atlanta I'd imagined the excitement of the girls. What would happen when I returned out of the blue? How shocked would they be that I'd held up my end of the bargain? Would they even still be there?

I'd traveled so far and told so many people about them. I had called in countless favors from family and friends to help. I had watched customers pause at the counter of my shop to read my note and then toss in the extra change from their lattes. I'd researched what things to bring, the educational system, women's rights in India, flight bargains, and translations of certain Hindi, Nepali, and Bengali phrases.

And now I am back, knocking on the big steel doors. I see an eye peek out of the crack and hear some rustling. Tiny feet shuffle back and forth, and then I hear one of the housemothers being summoned to get the key and unlock the door. This seems to take forever, but when the doors finally swing open, the whole orphanage is present and smiling at me. I want to crumble into a million pieces. I've made it back.

There, among the smiling faces, are the oldest three. They are still here. Still safe. I am relieved beyond words. They envelop me in a group hug, a wave of smiles, and hands reaching in to touch me. I fight back a waterfall of tears.

I wiggle my hands through the group and grab the three, the ones I have put so much thought into. These are the oldest three I've pledged to protect, to find them a place of safety and security when they have to leave the orphanage. As I draw them close, I am surprised that they don't seem shocked. They are happy to see me, for sure, but they aren't shocked.

"Are you surprised? Are you surprised I came back?" I ask.

They shake their heads with a very confused no.

"No? Not even a little?" I say with a squinty-eyed smile.

Labuki speaks for all of them: "No. You said you would come back, and you are the only person who said they would."

※

Over the next few days I meet with Jampa, the monk who runs the orphanage. He is sympathetic but his hands are tied. He barely has enough funding to keep the orphanage running, much less offer assistance to my far-fetched-sounding plan. There is so much poverty in this town that it's impossible to ask for help for these girls when there are thousands in the same—or worse—situations. Stories abound of lower-caste children who turn up dead or go missing. By comparison, my three have it pretty good.

Darjeeling is beautiful, but it is also cold and poverty-stricken. There are long stretches when the locals have no electricity or water. Paper signs advertising HIV testing clinics and discounted TB medications are plastered on buildings. The hospital has cold, stark rooms with little to no equipment. Any materials and goods in the hill town and surrounding villages have to be brought up one truckload at a time. The markets can be grim. Some farmers lay out a blue tarp on the ground to sell their goods, which may consist of only six withered potatoes or a handful of bruised okra.

Darjeeling has also been a hotbed of political strife for many years. Maoist groups used the region as a home base, touching off violent demonstrations. Around the time of my first trip, a local political official was decapitated while addressing a crowd in the town square.

Tribal protests have also riddled the area with unrest. Self-immolation and hunger strikes are not uncommon. And the upheaval has often led to months-long roadblocks, bringing tourism to a standstill and sealing the town from the outside world. It's these types of unfortunate circumstances that have brought some of these girls to this orphanage and have kept this mountain town from reaching its full potential.

I am staying for six weeks and have a laundry list of things to do. The first is to find some kind of living space close enough to town so the girls can keep attending the schools where they are enrolled. This is more complicated than it might appear. In India, you live with your parents, sometimes long after you are grown. People rarely move around or away from the place where they were born. The sons stay in the family house and the daughters live with their husband's family. Most houses in Darjeeling are occupied by generations of families that have lived there practically since the beginning of time.

In the United States, you would, of course, call a real estate agent, look in the paper or online, or even drive around looking for signs. In Darjeeling, it's not that easy. There are no classified ads or Craigslist postings. It's all done by word of mouth and only in quiet circles of same-caste groups. I ask around but hit only dead ends.

After a week of pestering anyone I can find, I start to get nervous. Manoj, Labuki, Devna, and I spend the next few nights wandering around the streets after dark looking for buildings with no lights inside, suggesting no one lives there. We write down notes on the location and come back the next day to ask if the place is vacant. This goes on for ten days. After a relentless search, we finally have some luck come our way. The owner of a local shop has a small apartment in his house available. A teacher from a local college had rented it until he got married and moved back to his village with his new wife into his parents' home.

The shop owner and his wife are kindhearted, but he is also a businessman. He asks for the first six months in rent upfront, not that unusual in India. The house gate is locked every night at 8:00 PM and opens back up at 6:00 AM, when their servants arrive to prepare for the day. It feels safe.

The apartment is small. There are two rooms, one for sleeping and the other for eating, praying, and studying. There is a tiny kitchen attached, but it doesn't come with a stove or any kind of refrigeration. Refrigerators are actually pretty rare in Darjeeling, and if you have one, it's usually the size of a small dorm room minifridge. People here don't eat many refrigerated items, and they only purchase what they are going to eat for that meal. Butter is really expensive and milk comes in a tiny ziplock bag straight from the cow.

I put down the deposit and sign the lease. I am not allowed to sign my own name, so I use my father's instead. India doesn't find weight in a woman's signature. I don't tell my dad.

We have a local advisor review the documents and give them an approval stamp.

I am feeling great. The owner of the house and his wife are good people; they are well known in the community as respected elders.

I tell the girls we will move the next morning.

We walk around town to find Sherpas to move the girls' belongings into the new apartment. Sherpas, members of the Tibetan tribe, are best known to Westerners for carrying the gear of mountain climbers and hikers in the Himalayan region (especially Mount Everest), but the term is also used for those who ferry things around the city with a thick canvas strap slung around their back but weighed down by their heads. Because Darjeeling is "walking only," this is the way most things get moved from place to place. I find two male Sherpas and ask them to meet us at the orphanage the following day.

The next morning I meet the Sherpas outside the orphanage, ready to pick up the girls' belongings. The girls look confused. I tell them to start bringing their stuff down to the front door so the men can begin carrying the things to our new apartment.

They go upstairs, and in five minutes, they are back. Between the three of them they have:

1. One pink shirt that was originally attached to a skirt, but the skirt has rotted away. It has netted cap sleeves with a thin band of fabric at the bottom of the netting. All of the netting has been worn away so just the trim on the sleeves is attached under the arms.

2. Two pairs of very old underwear.

3. A bunch of frayed papers with crayon drawings.

4. A photograph of Manoj and her brother.

5. School uniforms.

6. The photos I left with them on the first trip.

7. Every piece of paper I had drawn, written anything on, or doodled on from six months ago, neatly folded in a piece of cloth.

That's it. I tell the Sherpas we won't need their help after all, and we walk to the new space to settle in.

After dropping off their few belongings, with a notepad in hand, we are on our way through town with our list of necessities. We need the basics: a bed, mattress, sheets, minor household items, and kitchen stuff. We have to purchase a stove and put one of their IDs and a deposit down for a government-rationed propane tank.

I have them make the list of necessities for the house and negotiate the prices at the market. They love this. Not the things, really, but the idea of being in a position to negotiate. They also love walking through town with items in a bag. The idea that people are seeing these lowest-caste girls—who weren't even allowed to use some of the public bathrooms—carrying bought goods through the town in front of a high-caste people is a thrilling experience.

But the thing they are most excited about is school supplies. Topping the list is a dictionary and their own notebooks, a set of pencils in a long metal box, and their own books to bring home from their classes.

I set up a food ration account with a local shopkeeper and deposit enough money to last for six months. I purchase a pre-paid phone with a long-distance plan and plug my number into it. For years, it is the only number in the phone, because I'm the only person they know who has a phone. I give the landlord money for electricity and water delivery every week. I take them to their first trip to the doctor and ob-gyn, whose office is a room off of a local hotel lobby. I go to their schools and tell the teachers what's going on. I pay for upcoming school and test fees and purchase everything on their supply list.

I have two remaining weeks here to watch them settle in. I know for Americans this sounds crazy, to leave three seventeen-year-old girls on their own and trust that they will do the right thing. But these girls know this is a chance of a lifetime, and they are not going to let anything screw this up.

These are also girls who have never failed a grade. With no real motivation to do well in school, they have anyway. Even with no promise of a good future, they are at the top of their class. There are other girls in the orphanage who are twelve and thirteen years old and still in the second and third grade. That's not uncommon. Nearly one out of every two girls in India drops out of school by fifth grade. These girls have been given a window of opportunity and can see the sunlight bursting in.

By this second trip, I have met people in town—shopkeepers who sell us the supplies for the apartment, travel agents who book my tickets, local Sherpas who deliver our things, people who work at the school supply store, their teachers, and local homeowners who we approached about renting rooms. Word spreads pretty quickly within the community about what I am doing. At every end of the city, there is a set of eyes on these girls, and every place we go, I introduce myself. Sometimes the person stops me and says, "I already know who you are: orphanage girl-child-helper lady who feeds dogs."

On my final day, we have a long talk about being responsible. I remind them to be very respectful to the house owners, to conserve the electricity that runs from the main house, and to be mindful of their water usage.

Water is the hottest commodity in Darjeeling. The water delivery truck only comes once a week. The truck fills up a small tub on the roof that homeowners pull their water from via a hose for cooking, washing, and bathing. Sometimes water is unavailable for weeks. This can cause many medical problems in the town when people seek an alternative water source. Any water that is delivered is run-off rainwater or comes from a local man-made reserve. The water has to be boiled before using because of contamination from waterborne diseases.

Before it seems possible, my six weeks is up and it's time to return home. I am rounding up our to-do list and regrettably counting the days until my departure.

As I'm packing, I overhear the girls discussing something and I can tell it's a secret. I lean in to eavesdrop and they stop.

"Who are you talking about?" I ask. "Who do you call Tiger Heart?"

"You!" they say in unison. "*You* are the Tiger Heart."

Manoj continued, "You are fierce and will pounce but you are also protective and you have yellow hair." They all giggle. I am humbled and in awe of my girls.

I hug the girls a million times. I remind them that they have my phone number, and I promise that in six months, I'll be back.

Chapter 10

THE SECOND
TIME AROUND

> "These are the days that must
> happen to you."
>
> —Walt Whitman

ack at home, I show my customers the letters I receive from the girls and update them on their progress. For a time, things seem stable. But then I receive some devastating news and my world suddenly slams to a screeching halt. I get the phone call that no one wants to receive.

I learn that my mom has been diagnosed with stage-four brain cancer. She has battled migraines throughout her life, so when things got worse, she thought she was just having a particularly bad "spell."

Without much warning, we are told by her doctor that she only has a couple of months to live. We should start to prepare, the doctor says, and find my dad a grief support group.

It's a huge shock. I realize at this moment that my parents are human, not immortal. And I begin to grieve the loss of my mom even as she's sitting right in front of me. The grief worms itself into every minute of my day, every pause in every conversation.

I catch myself going about my day as usual, and then it hits me, immobilizing that minute, which turns into hours.

The grief is for my mom but also for my dad. My parents have been married my entire life. They do everything together. They are a unit. They bitch about the same things, have the same friends, and are pretty much connected at the hip. I can't imagine my dad being alone, sitting in the living room that my mom decorated, staring at the tchotchkes balanced on a little wooden shelf that says "The Christies."

After weeks of driving back and forth to my parents' house and to doctors' appointments, they tell us that the only thing they can offer is a round of chemo. It will start in a couple of weeks, and it might add a month or so to her life. She's already a different person. Her face is swollen from the steroids she's taking. She slurs her speech when she answers questions. Lethargic, she sleeps all the time.

The night before her first chemo appointment, my dad calls and asks, in a monotone voice, if I'm coming to the hospital in the morning. I say yes and climb into bed early, feeling gutted. In the morning, while I'm getting ready, my dad calls again and says Mom's doctor's wife had twins the night before. The chemo session is postponed.

That's it. Every piece of me that I'd been carefully holding together with deep breaths for months explodes. My father is numb. He has moved far past the fight. But I'm just getting started. And I can't conceive of asking someone who only has a few weeks to live to wait even a minute longer for treatment that could help.

I start Googling every doctor and hospital in Atlanta, hunting for the best. One doctor at Emory has reviews that are off the charts. I need to get my mom into treatment quickly because that would mean we were working on something, that we had some plan, that we didn't have to focus on the end, just the process.

The next morning we are in the office of the "best doctor." I've had her x-rays rushed over and he's reviewed her records. He's talking but I can't hear him. I'm concentrating on my mom, who is foggy and teetering in her seat. My brain is filtering out anything but "let's start chemo now." That's what I am waiting to hear.

He asks if we have any more questions, and I realize I haven't heard any plan. I haven't heard anything at all, just a big bunch of big medical phrases I don't understand. My parents get up to walk out and I ask "best doctor" if we can speak in private. My dad shuffles my frail mom out to the waiting room and we sit back down.

"Okay," I say to the doctor. "You don't have to sugarcoat this for me. We already know, so just give it to me straight."

He sits there calmly as I keep talking.

"My question is, I have this project in India. It's not a question of *if* I go back but *when*. This isn't a hobby, it's a commitment. I am fully responsible for a whole slew of young women in Darjeeling. I go every six months and that is mandatory. They have no one else. Should I go now or should I wait? How long do we have?"

I am numb. I am devastated. But I also have a houseful of young women depending on me. I'd like to curl up in bed for six months, but that simply isn't possible.

The doctor looks at me and shakes his head.

"I have no idea. That's up to you."

"Well, if we have three months, I'll wait. If we have five months I'll go now and stay long enough to register them for school and come right back."

He pauses for a moment and then says, "Your mom is going to be fine. She is scheduled for brain surgery tomorrow morning. We are removing two tumors. And with the other two, we are going to put her in the gamma knife machine and disintegrate them."

I don't believe him. I think that he saw my eagerness to pummel something or someone and tells me this fairy tale to keep me from losing my shit.

The next morning while she's in the operating room, I wait for the results along with my dad and their friends.

We sit for hours in a lifeless hospital waiting room.

I don't tell my dad what the doctor said because I am still convinced he was only trying to calm me down. When "best doctor" comes out and tells us that things looked great, I still don't breathe. And I didn't breathe for quite some time.

It's now been four years since my mom was deemed cancer free. It took two brain surgeries, a round of chemo, and some visits under the gamma knife, which was an experimental procedure at the time.

Her last checkup showed that a few bad cells have appeared in her lungs, even though she's never smoked a day in her life. They've put her on minimal treatment, and we all have a great outlook since they caught things so soon.

To say that facing death had a profound influence on our family would be an understatement. My parents have been doing all the things they had always talked about. They've traveled to Scotland to trace their roots. They've taken a riverboat cruise and hiked to a cabin in the Appalachians. There is barely a week that goes by that they don't jump in the car and drive off like giddy teenagers to some cool place or another.

I once saw a quote that said, "What if the cure for cancer is locked in someone's brain who can't afford an education?"

What if.

Chapter 11

THE HOUSE ON UP-UP ROAD

"You've always had the power,
my dear, you just had to
learn it for yourself."

—Glinda the Good Witch, *The Wizard of Oz*

 am back in Darjeeling. Years have passed since my first trip to the orphanage. I've been to India dozens of times now. This country has become familiar to me, and I have nearly as many friends here as I do back in Atlanta.

The project has grown.

We are sitting around the table for dinner. A mound of rice and a scoop of spicy potatoes are piled on metal plates. An individual bowl of yellow dal sits on the side. Everyone has their small cup of water. But I have a big bottle that I take swigs from throughout the meal so I can survive the spicy bites. They find this funny.

The walls are cream-colored but our drapes are pink with big, darker pink flowers. One table isn't enough at this point, so I've bought a second, and we've lined them up, end to end.

At dinner we go around the table and each girl volunteers one thing she learned that day. There are twelve of us now, including

Nisha, our housemother, and me. We hear stories of a new bird species, weather reports, kind gestures from school friends. As we wind our way around the long table, Rabani—an orphan whose parents have both died from tuberculosis in the last two years—takes her turn. She is impish, bubbly, and scary smart.

"Today, our teacher told us about the number zero, which has no worth," she says.

"But put it next to another number, and it makes that number important. The more zeros you add, the bigger the number gets. So know that if you are feeling like a zero, you do have great worth with teamwork."

We have two honey-colored cats that you can find curled up on someone's pink bed. The girls named them Biscuit and Gravy in honor of my Southern roots. Most of the bedsheets, comforters, and curtains are pink with fringe or sequins or ruffles. The girly decor is their choice. I want them to have some nice things that are their own. All the girls have photos or drawings from school taped around their beds. Some have different religious figures—Hindu, Buddhist, Muslim, Christian. We don't discriminate. This project is about education, not religion.

The house we rent has three bedrooms, a living room, a long dining room, and a detached kitchen. We have a patio out front where all the girls sit and study on rare sunny days. We have some small plants in clay pots we maintain for the landlord.

The house is tan, with a big yellow door, but it looks pink when the sunlight hits it just right. It sits at the top of a hill on what the locals call the Up-Up road.

It's been a long journey to get here. It hasn't been easy.

After some trial and error, I figured out that the best way to keep a steady stream of money flowing into the program so we could pay the bills was to hold a monthly fund-raising dinner featuring Indian dishes at Dr. Bombay's, my tea shop back in Atlanta. This has been great, but every month it's a big commitment. Some dinners sell out. Others draw just the regulars. But no matter how much we take in, the bills still come due. The dinners don't pay the whole tab. The shop—through the patronage of our loyal customers—makes up the difference.

Early on, I decided to focus my efforts on college-age girls. So many organizations are helping younger women in India, but I saw a big gap when it came to helping them make their way to college and a professional career that would allow them to dream big. In my mind it would also help stop the vicious cycle of poverty for them. Hopefully, a college degree could enable them to work and help them put their own girls through college when they become mothers. It would be a safety net for them if they found themselves in bad relationships and had to make it on their own. Education is freedom in the world, but in India, it can mean the difference between life and death.

When I started out, the girls were attending cheaper government colleges. But their success has meant they've been accepted into more prestigious and expensive private schools. As tiny and isolated as Darjeeling is, it has several small local colleges. The girls have also begun taking part in a lot more extracurricular activities, which come at a cost.

There have been setbacks, but we've made it through. We've moved three times. Once it was because we outgrew our space.

Another time our landlord decided he was hiking the rent to seven times what we were paying. He did this after Googling me and discovering that I owned a store in the United States. He must've figured he could squeeze more money out of me and take severe advantage of the situation. This sleazy landlord also assumed we would pay. He was shocked when I found a new place within twenty-four hours and didn't even bother to entertain his demands. This sent a message that echoed throughout the town.

I've received a lot of support from local folks and different organizations. I have befriended strong Indian women in high places. They have helped and mentored me along the way. Like me, they believe in the girl child in a culture that still marginalizes girls and women.

One of the newest girls to join the Learning Tea was one of the younger kids at the orphanage when I made my first visit to Darjeeling. After we put down roots and became somewhat established, I returned to the orphanage and put an offer on the table. I told the girls there that if they got good grades, kept their schoolwork up, and wanted to go to college, I would bust my can to give them a scholarship to make that happen. The attitude toward school has changed drastically around the orphanage.

At the time, this girl was a failing student. But she turned it around. She worried constantly about her future. When she came into the house, she was very quiet and very intimidated. But she is a different person now—superconfident, with a lot to say at our dinner discussions. She's also pretty dang funny. Her mother is mentally ill and still wanders the town.

All the young women in the program have responsibilities. Believe it or not, they actually love these. This program is not a free ride; it's a leg up. The housemother is not a maid or a cook. She keeps our finances in order, pays the bills on time, and attends school meetings. She also monitors their volunteer work. Each girl in the program has to put in between ten and fifteen hours a month of volunteer time, depending on their school schedule. (Some girls have school six days a week.) They're allowed to volunteer anywhere they choose as long as they are helping others and not being paid.

Some girls volunteer to help elderly indigent residents prepare food. Some go on trips to help care for animals at farms in isolated villages or tutor the children of domestic workers. Others work with the street dogs program, washing and vaccinating dogs.

On my first trip to Darjeeling, I was struck by the villagers' compassion when it came to animals. In the morning, almost every house had a metal dinner plate of leftovers sitting on the ground outside the front door for the local street dogs. Even though goods were scarce and food was expensive, people cared enough to feed the packs of hungry dogs that roamed Darjeeling.

The volunteerism is the most important part of the program for me because it allows the girls to take the opportunity they've received and pay it forward. It also earns them respect in the community where, not so long ago, they'd been dismissed as next to nothing. For some folks in Darjeeling, meeting one of my students out there helping may be the first contact they've had with a lower-caste girl, so the girls are ambassadors. I had a local women's handicraft group make the girls green scarves with a signature tea leaf embroidered on one end that they wear when they volunteer, so they're easily recognized.

I want them to stay in India, but if their dreams and education take them somewhere else, that is their choice. But becoming role models and giving back in their own communities is the grand plan, hopefully, for some. India needs more strong women, and young girls in India need to hear about success stories of orphans or slum children or girls turned over by families who did not want the girl child. The girls there are hungry for the opportunity to succeed.

To stay in the program the girls also have to earn passing grades. If they fail once, they are on academic probation; if they fail again, they are out of the program and have to move out of the house.

Through the years, I've come to realize that it's good to have expectations; to decide what your rules are and stick with them. You can't help everyone and you can't make people take your help. They have to want it. You can't force these young women to go to college. That might not be their path. Some girls their age in the villages in the area already have two or three kids. The Learning Tea isn't about dictating what a girl should do with her life; rather, it's about giving some of them a choice by offering them the tools they need to go forward with college if that's what they want.

Early on in the project, one of the original three older girls from the orphanage dropped out. She simply didn't want to go to school. Instead, she wanted to be a dancer or a flight attendant (a job that in India is designed for young women only), so she ended up moving to a village to live with her uncle. For a long time, I sat up nights worrying about her, but eventually, I had to come to peace with it. Just because you swoop in with money or opportunity doesn't mean that what you're offering is right for everyone.

The girls also can't get married while they're in the program. This rule is mostly aimed at any remaining family members. Some of the girls still have a surviving relative or two. With others there is a whole family that gave them up because of their gender. Arranged marriage is still the norm in India. So this rule is a promise between their relatives and me that the student won't be taken out of school and out of the program for marriage.

It's hard to believe, but these young women—in their late teens or early twenties—aren't boy crazy in the same way Americans their age often are. They watch the occasional Bollywood music video on TV while we eat pizza at Darjeeling's only pizza place, but, in general, they are far more into Disney movies, like *Frozen* or *High School Musical*.

The girls also do all their own cooking and maintain the house. Each week they make a group grocery list with their budget, and a different girl goes to the market to shop. They take turns preparing dinner, and it can get a little competitive as they try to earn bragging rights for "best cook."

Labuki, one of the first young women who came into the program, has taken over tracking the finances and is doing an amazing job. She and I share a love of spreadsheets. Most of the girls are already closing in on a career they want to pursue. But Labuki has expressed interest in helping to open another Learning Tea center in another city in India. She's our mama hen.

These young women are excelling beyond everyone's expectations. One is in teacher's college and has been selected to be the teacher's aide, a coveted top spot. Another won admission to one of the most prestigious women's colleges in Darjeeling, which was founded by Mother Teresa's nuns. Two have been selected from their school to march in front of the president of India. There is a soccer team captain in the house. Another transformed her failing grades into straight As after we bought her a pair of glasses. Two of them are currently applying for their master's degrees. There is a violinist and a cellist. I could go on and on. I am insanely proud of them. There is a huge success story that follows each one of these young women.

We do hair and paint nails. A lot of time here is spent washing and fluffing Biscuit and Gravy. On one of my trips, I brought one of those hair bun makers from Atlanta, and they were mesmerized by it. We had to make a chart of who could use it on certain days. I got frustrated, so I went to the market and bought some pot scrubbers and some black socks, rolled out the pot scrubbers and covered them in the socks, and made all the girls a bun maker of their own. Now they all have huge Princess Leia buns. I love Darjeeling and I love my extended family. When I am here, I usually roll out of bed around 8:00 AM. The ladies have usually been up since five. Before I've even opened my eyes, they've typically studied for at least an hour, washed and hung out their clothes, eaten breakfast, and made lunch to bring with them to school.

If you ask anyone in town where we live, they say, "That's Tiger Heart's house with the Learning Tea students on the Up-Up road."

Chapter 12

BEAUTIFUL DISASTER— VIGNETTES FROM INDIA

> "Go sell crazy someplace else.
> We're all stocked up here."
>
> —Jack Nicholson as Melvin Udall
> in *As Good as It Gets*

People *always ask me to describe India.* Picture a large group of men dressed in orange dancing through the streets behind a blaring speaker in the back of a dump truck. A wild mother pig and her piglets come trotting down a busy street—with a monkey riding on her back. You drive through the desert and stumble upon a man sitting alone on a box with a sign that says "fax" and there sits a typewriter, connected to nothing.

India is gorgeous and tragic and humbling all blended into one, and I can't get enough of its surprises. I have sat on my bed in India at different times on different trips and rationed out my Q-tips. I'm exhausted by the idea that I might have to haul ass over a herd of goats; nine naked, sleeping babies; six piles of cow poo; forty dogs; a basket of live chickens; and hashed-out, snake-charming soothsayers so that I can jump a moving train that either came a day late or left three minutes too early.

I actually remember breaking all my Q-tips in half to conserve space. I don't carry anything that I don't need to use every day. Everything in my luggage is mandatory.

Part 1: Raja from Mumbai

On this particular trip, my flight has been rescheduled through another airline, so I'm waiting in Mumbai. Mumbai is so crowded that it takes hours to go inches. Everything is bumper-to-bumper. Every taxi is fighting to squeeze into any small opening in traffic. Move two inches, honk sixteen times, then do it all over again for miles. The airport is only about sixteen miles from my hotel, but I have to reserve at least two and a half hours to get there.

My American friends marvel that with all the crazy driving, India must have horrible wrecks, but I have never seen a real wreck here. Two cars rolling together, yes. Having the end of my cigarette lopped off in traffic because the neighboring car was so close, check. Almost being driven off a cliff Thelma and Louise–style to avoid hitting an animal, yes. An older lady falling out of a sitting rickshaw, yup. But after traveling thousands of miles in this country, never a wreck. You rarely get going fast enough to cause any real damage. It's kind of like playing bumper cars.

One day, I have a meeting in Bandra, about a seven-mile trip, which in Mumbai time translates into an hour-plus journey. I hail a taxi and a small Indian man with dark skin, a white beard, and thick, brown, Coke-bottle glasses welcomes me into his 1950s Ambassador. He is in his early seventies, wearing a pressed, clean, white kurta and MC Hammer–type pants. He opens the door for me and tells me his name is Raja, which means "prince" in Hindi.

I give him loose directions and we are off, like molasses. He is cramming his tiny taxi into any space available, like stuffing a marshmallow into a piggy bank, and honking violently.

Since most taxis here don't have radios, I always travel with small speakers.

On long taxi rides, I like to bridge the communication gap by deejaying from my iPod. This usually humors my driver and keeps my fare low. I sing, and sometimes they sing every tenth word that rhymes, and we crawl across the country together in song.

I put my iPod on shuffle. We sing some Bowie. We sing MGMT. We sing the theme song to *Annie*. He smiles at me in his rearview mirror and I smile back. We are both singing at the top of our lungs. He has no idea what he is singing, but he already has the tune down, and I can tell he thinks we are funny.

At complete stops he looks around to see if anyone is watching this odd two-person circus act going on in his taxi. He sings louder.

For one and a half hours, we are friends. Great friends. We laugh. We sing. We play pranks on each other. He swerves the car and thinks I will find that funny (I don't). He smacks a rag on top of the car to the beat of the music. He does a little jazz hands at one point and other dance moves I call "turn the lightbulb" and "feed the chickens."

He offers me some dingy, brown water out of an old, crinkled water bottle that has been rolling back and forth on the floorboard. He points out the photos of his family he has covering the speedometer above his steering wheel: his wife, children, and grandchildren. He lights up as he points to a photo of a baby; the edges of the photo are brown and peeling.

I start playing what I think he will like. He has a few bobble-head Hindu gods mounted on his dashboard, so I dig up some Bollywood music.

Then, as suddenly as it began, it ends—and we break up. I get out of the car, give him his money, smile, and head off to my meeting.

Three hours later, I leave and walk back outside to look for my next deejay victim. I hail another cab.

We stop at a red light and a motorcycle pulls up beside me. On it are a dad and five little girls in their school uniforms, all on one motorbike. One of them—wedged between two others—is fast asleep. They smile and wave. I reach for my camera and nothing. No camera.

I tell my driver to make a quick U-turn and I run back into the building where I had the meeting. We look everywhere. No camera. No sign of my camera. The last time I remember my camera, I was in the taxi with Raja. Shit! Shit! Shit!

That camera has been an extension of my arm for years now. That camera has defended my honor when people have doubted what they think are tall tales and far-fetched stories I bring back from India.

I am at a loss, deflated.

My taxi arrives back at my hotel and I shuffle in, drop my things, and tear up. I know there is no way I can repurchase my camera here, and I have so many more pictures I need to take.

I go outside in search of a chai and start wandering the streets of Mumbai. I walk down to the same place where I met Raja and nothing.

Raja and my thousand-dollar Nikon are off celebrating. Hopefully he will cash it in and feed his family or fix the drooping felt on his taxi ceiling. Maybe he will be inspired to purchase some speakers so he can flash mob Mumbai with his high-pitched voice and his newfound love for songs from *Annie*.

The camera is long gone. He has no way of finding me, and I am devastated.

Walking back, I think I see another driver who was standing beside Raja when I was getting in the cab. He only has one eye, so I know it's him. I start asking him about Raja.

"Yes, yes, very short, long white kurta, thick glasses; his name is RAAAAAJJJJAAAAAAA; he is Hindu," I say.

The one-eyed man looks perplexed, but he is thinking. He waves his hands, "Not Raja: Mohamed."

"No, definitely not Mohamed," I insist. "His name was Raja. He is Hindu. He has little glitter Ganesh statues glued to his dashboard. They have some fake silk flowers glued to them too. His name is definitely not Mohamed."

I tell him we are talking about different drivers and start to walk away. But then he describes him one more time, to a T.

He tells me that Mohamed goes by Raja. He glues Hindu gods in his car and wears a dot on his head because otherwise Western tourists will pass him by because he is Muslim. He says that since 9-11, Muslim drivers who cater to tourists sit for hours with no fares, and that a lot of Muslims pretend to be Hindu in order to get Western business to feed their families and keep the jobs they have had for years. Mohamed has to do this to look more like "friends," he says. I can't think of a friendlier man than Raja.

I trudge the three blocks back to my hotel and my camera is there. According to the luggage boy, it has been there for an hour. He tells me a taximan was walking hotel to hotel looking for the lady with big yellow hair and—then he puffed up his cheeks to imply that I am chubby.

He hands me my camera, and he and his friend laugh hysterically and run out into the street.

Part 2: Magic Sing Karaoke Machine

I am still waiting in Mumbai for my new ticket. The now bankrupt airline I purchased my ticket from has passed me on to a working airline, and I have a few days to kill before my next flight. I am tired and frustrated. The costs are piling up, and I am eager to get to Darjeeling and see the Learning Tea girls. Mumbai is eating up my days away from the tea shop, and I can only afford to pay someone to work my shifts for so long.

When people hear you own a business, they think you drive a fancy Lexus or lounge by a pool in Bora Bora with a standard poodle named Jacques. I am here to tell you that if that is what being a business owner looks like, I have made some bad decisions and taken some wrong turns.

But I love my job. I love my leafy little neighborhood where I know most of my customers by name. I love making sweets that people enjoy. I love seeing little kids' faces when they walk in, wide-eyed, and see my bevy of colorful junk. Maybe I should've sold Amway or Mary Kay, so I could be riding around town in a pink Cadillac instead of my twelve-year-old Honda. Instead, I have bided my time in more hotels in India than I can remember, waiting for credit card batches to go through at the store back in Atlanta so I can pay my hotel bill.

On this particular night, I am trying to check my bank balance, but the hotel Wi-Fi is a no-show. So I head to the nearest bar to get a cold one. This is where I meet Anil and Rajiv. They are both in their late thirties, both married, and both in fights with their wives. They are also self-proclaimed spokesmen for a world-renowned "couch-surfing" website, where you offer a guest room, extra couch, a blow-up mattress, or even a dirty corner of your living room to low-budget travelers lugging backpacks.

I can immediately tell this is the single-most exciting thing that has ever happened to either one of these men. They are physically high off the magnificent stories of all-night dance parties, bong hits, snowboarding, solo trekking, extreme trance deejay mixes, hash running, and horoscope card readings from these world travelers.

Their camera phones are overflowing with images of Euro-Russian girls with bad blond dye jobs who had slept on their living room floor among their kids' cheap plastic toys, some pillows, and worn flip-flops.

The pictures show young women in inappropriate outfits posing amid their very annoyed-looking wives and their bewildered children. One shows a smiling French girl in a tube top and mini skirt sitting with the family at the dinner table. Rajiv's wife hovers in the background with the most angry, eat-shit look I have ever seen.

I'm not sure this pair is really interested in talking to me so much as using me as a panel judge for the coveted photo array of ladies they have had "couch surf" at their apartments over the last three months.

For four and a half hours I am graced with all the "oh so cute" things these modern traveling ladies said, did, or wore at their houses. Once or twice, to catch their breath, they ask me why I am in India and, once or twice, I get in about three sentences about my project before one of them suddenly starts giggling while recounting something cute "Latvia" said or wore.

Then they pull their camera phones out and pore over their catalog of couch-surfing ladies all over again. When the drinks run out at the bar, I pass both of them my card. Before they leave, we promise to be best friends forever, keep in touch, and maybe have dinner with their families when their relationships with their wives improve.

The next day, while I'm still waiting in Mumbai for my flight to be rescheduled, I receive a text: "Come to Rajiv's house for dinner, please, please, please," it says.

"Sorry, I'm busy," I text back.

"Please!" comes the reply. "We have something for you."

I call Rajiv and try to worm my way out of it, but he's having none of it. His wife has cooked her family dish. He's already told his kids and they are all coming to pick me up at my hotel at 6:15 in a very small taxi.

Finally, I say yes. I give a few guests at the hotel the name of the couch-surfing website, just in case. When Rajiv and his family members arrive, I have the hotel owner come out to the taxi with me. I size them up and quickly surmise that I could probably fend them off if things took a bad turn. I hop in. I figure I can jump out at a red light if things get hairy.

I'm served a beautiful meal in a very modest and small apartment on the edge of the slums. They buy a beer for all of us to share and produce one very coveted chocolate Philly blunt cigar still in its original packaging. One of the couch surfers left it behind. We talk for a while. His wife is warmed over by my poor attempt at Hindi, my stories of Darjeeling, and, mostly, my long pants.

I am about to leave but they stop me.

"Wait, wait, we have a gift."

I'd almost forgotten, and, quite frankly, the generous home-cooked meal on their budget would have been more than enough.

They drag out two huge plastic shopping bags. Everyone is on the edge of their seats, giddy, giggling, and wiggling. The kids are nervously hopping from one foot to the other, smiling and wringing their hands. One is twirling my hair, waiting patiently for me to open this present. They are trying not to pounce on me like little tigers and open it themselves.

I peel back the plastic, and . . . drumroll . . . inside the bags are a brand-new portable DVD player and a really fantastic Magic Sing Karaoke Machine. They tell me their family saves up every year to do one charitable thing. After reviewing the Learning Tea website and seeing how desperate the situation is, they obviously chose this. They also bought nine hundred extra songs that translate from Hindi to English to help the girls work on their language.

I am humbled by India, its culture, its people, and their relentless ability to surprise me with their kindness.

So now I am carrying twenty-four Q-tips, my suitcase, the DVD player with detachable screen, and a huge Magic Sing Karaoke Machine with a bonus pack deejay microphone stand for duets.

Soon after this evening, my plane ticket is finally delivered to my hotel. I close my bill and tell the staff I will be on my way. They ask me to answer the reception desk phone one more time in a fake British accent, which they love. The owner gets up and comes out to hug me and wish me luck. He apologizes once more for the crows.

When I had initially rented the room, I asked to see it first. When the owner opened the door, half a dozen crows were hopping around on the bed. He tried to shoo them out the open window but saw my face as they squawked loudly.

"Wrong room," he said.

We got on the elevator. He made a call in Hindi. We rode up, then back down to the same floor. I saw the hotel staff briskly walking out of the same room as before. He opened the same door as he had earlier, but this time the window was closed and there were no crows.

"Best room," he said. I took it.

But today, I say my good-byes in the dark and stop to tell the one-eyed man sleeping in his taxi that I think Raja is the greatest man that ever lived. Then I'm off.

Part 3: Holi Hell

The trip to Darjeeling goes something like this:

- ✓ 4:00 AM wake up
- ✓ Two hours to the airport (which is just sixteen miles away)

✓ Seven-hour flight across India with three layovers
✓ Land at Bagdogra Airport around 1:00 PM

From the airport I hire a driver with a giant 4×4 Land Cruiser to haul me and my stuff six hours up into the Himalayas to Darjeeling. Because of the dangerous roads and mud slides, drivers will not take you there in the dark, so the schedule is tight.

My driver's name is Bebeswa. He speaks about six English words. He is so tiny he can barely see over the steering wheel. He is looking for a gas station. We drive about three miles and I start to see the other passengers from my flight—mostly Indian families—sitting on the side of the road beside their suitcases.

Bebeswa pulls into a gas station with a growing crowd. Everyone wants gas. They are rattling the metal gate that holds the front of the store together. Apparently, all gas stations are closed due to the holiday.

India has a lot of holidays. In West Bengal, it is Holi Day, the festival to ring in spring. They celebrate this by dancing, throwing colored chalk at each other, and drinking as soon as the sun comes up. There is also a lot of hash smoking.

Bebeswa bounds out of the Land Cruiser. He doesn't say "wait" or "hold on" or "bye." He doesn't say a word.

I see him rush into the crowd, and then I see his tiny head disappear. I sit in the car for more than an hour waiting for him to emerge from the throng of purple, pink, and green chanting people. They are mostly men and mostly very drunk, so I don't get out of the car.

After an hour and a half, Bebeswa appears again, visibly wasted. He says gas is coming. I know gas is not coming because people are leaving. There are four men passed out drunk where the crowd once was. Two other tiny Indian men are swinging each other in circles with their hands locked, twirling down the street.

My time is running out before I get stuck here in the middle of nowhere.

So I give Bebeswa the option to take me back to the airport or I call the police; he takes me back to the airport.

Back at the airport, Bebeswa gets into a fight with the man from the taxi company who hired him. This man is in a kiosk with a tinted glass window and a small hole to talk through. As they argue, louder and louder, the taximan's hand reaches out through the hole. All I can see is the hand reaching out and smacking Bebeswa in the face.

There is more yelling, then the man informs me he has called his friend to open his gas station. Bebeswa and I climb back into the giant Land Cruiser and we are off. I am hoping he has sobered up, because there are no other options left at this point.

After going a short distance, we begin to slow down. The car starts to sputter. Bebeswa rocks violently back and forth in his seat, but still we roll to a stop. We walk with my luggage, the DVD player, the Magic Sing Karaoke Machine with dual microphone duet stand, and some things I picked up in Mumbai for the girls.

Bebeswa motions for me to start scavenging the streets for empty water bottles to hold gas. We collect about ten that don't have holes. Some kids see us doing this and think it's a game. They run ahead and grab the good ones first and run off.

At this new gas station, there is another line and another fight, and everyone thinks it's funny to cover me and all of my things in colored chalk powder. I don't think it's funny, but they are drunk and high out of their minds and think it's hilarious. Bebeswa fills our water bottles with gas and we start the slow walk toward a minivan taxi his friend has agreed to lend him that is smaller and gets better gas mileage.

Finally, we are threading our way up into the mountains, on our way to Darjeeling. We bounce, hitting every pothole, and I am thinking about a jog bra. We have driven for at least three hours.

We are swerving, and Bebeswa is gripping every curve with death-defying speed. Looking down, I can't even make out a building below. I am contemplating this sheer drop into the clouds when I hear a loud *pop*. The car stops. Bebeswa gets out, I get out. Bebeswa is crawling up under the minivan bus; I am crawling under the minivan bus. But it doesn't take a mechanic to see what's wrong. Bebeswa has busted the axle, which has broken completely in half with one end lying on the road.

A truck loaded down with chickens eases up next to us as the driver gapes at our predicament. Bebeswa frantically flags them down. The next thing I know, my things are being tossed into the open bed of the truck. I climb in behind and wave good-bye to Bebeswa. In the truck the radio is playing, "Do You Believe in Magic" by The Lovin' Spoonful. I am wedged in between live and dead chickens. Blowing feathers are stuck to my Chapstick. This ride takes about two hours.

It is dark when they drop me off at the taxi station; I schlep my enormous pile of stuff uphill through the town square and to our center. This day was hard.

The girls are superexcited to see me.

"How was your day?" they ask.

"Oh, it was good, how was yours?" I reply.

I hand them my iPad to watch *Tangled* and fall into bed. I can hear them in the other room watching the movie. They have never seen an iPad and look at it like it's a spaceship. As I fall asleep, I can hear them giggling and trying to sing along.

Chapter 13

PIÑA COLADAS FOR BREAKFAST

> "Let the wild rumpus start."
>
> —Maurice Sendak,
> *Where the Wild Things Are*

 am at my shop behind the counter. This woman in her early twenties comes in. She's wearing very little makeup, a T-shirt and jeans, and tennis shoes, and her hair pulled back in a ponytail.

She reaches the counter, and as I'm making her a latte, we start a conversation. I can barely hear her as I'm steaming the milk, but I get the gist. She's an intern for a local Fox TV station, and she wants to interview me about the Learning Tea.

"Sure," I tell her, and hand her my card. Then the next customer approaches.

A couple of weeks later, she e-mails me with questions and says she's bringing a camera guy. The day of the filming, my employee gets sick and I'm the only one working. The interview is going to have to happen between customers at the counter. Just by chance, my first patron is a girl who tips her entire mocha back on me while answering her phone.

I'm in the middle of the morning rush when the intern shows up with her small crew. We do the interview in between customers, me behind the counter. I'm completely nervous, but, due to the rush, I just don't have time to let my nerves get the best of me. I've done this before, no less than one hundred times. Some student, some parent, some Girl Scout troop, some ladies' book club, some class, some group from the old folks' home comes into the shop and wants me to say a few words. Every time it's equally nerve-racking. I spoke to a group of twelve five-year-olds once and I was nervous. To say I hate public speaking is an understatement.

Public speaking is my Achilles' heel. If I loved it, I would probably be in quite a different place right now, gabbing up the Learning Tea at some fancy conference and not counting dimes from the tip jar to pay for scholarships. Throw me in with a small group of friends, a drink in my hand, and I'm the life of the party. But put me in front of a crowd and I go completely stiff.

I usually get the same reaction: "It's not that bad, oh please, girl! You can do it. Oh come on. If I can do it, you can do it."

When people say that to me, I think to myself, *Okay, wait. I've dedicated my life and every penny I have to flying across the world by myself. I've made it through two armed robberies, one attempted carjacking at gunpoint, one knife holdup, and one hijacked train. I was smuggled through a political war zone in the hatchback of a car, covered in burlap. I've tossed on a burqa to be able to ride the train by myself. Throw in a handful of death threats. And then there's bullying from people who don't want my low-caste scholars to take seats away from their rich kids at school. Aren't I full up? Do I really have to get better at something else? Should I really spend my time*

worrying about the correct lipstick shade for a public appearance? Or
stress out over falling down on the way to some podium or forgetting
where I am in the story?

So back at the tea shop, they film the short piece. In between
cuts and customers, they hand me a napkin from the condiments
station and tell me to wipe the grease off my face. They ask me
to put on more makeup, which I don't have, and didn't know I
needed. I think I've made all my points but don't remember. I hope
I didn't sound like a complete idiot, and then they're gone.

Weeks go by, and I forget about it. I chalk it up to the intern
getting some experience under her belt. Then one morning, I get
a call from the producer. I am at my shop in the kitchen on the
floor trying to light the flame on the water heater.

"Hey, we're gonna air your story at noon," he says.

"Okay. That's cool, thanks."

I go back to working on the water heater. A few hours go by,
and I get another call.

"Hey, we're airing your story in one hour," he updates me.

"Um, okay. Thanks."

I wonder if he remembers calling me before. Nick, my business
partner, comes back from getting supplies, and I remind him of
that intern thing from a few weeks prior.

Noon hits and the show airs nationally. I'm working, so I can't
watch it. But I hear my phone going off with texts. Some are people wanting to go to India while others want me to contact their
friends in India. Some Indians say they want to come to my shop
for tea. And then there are the parents who want me to take their
bratty kids to India to show them what kids who don't have Xboxes

do with their time. On the segment, they tell viewers that if they want to help, they should go online and purchase my tea.

I sell packages of loose Darjeeling tea at my shop to raise money for the project. A local art school designed the labels as a class project four years ago. I've paid a tech at OfficeMax to update the information on the back as we've grown. This tea was a marketing tool and a fun project to work on with the class. It helps tell people what we're doing. It's a cute way to get our name into someone's hand. Any chance I get to donate a pack to a local school auction, I do.

But after the cost of the tea and the shipping from a tiny stall in Darjeeling, printing labels at OfficeMax, cutting them out, and taping the labels on ourselves, there is not a lot of money to be had.

One misconception of having a humanitarian project is that money is always flying at you; that every day you go to the mailbox and pull out a giant stack of checks from rich billionaires. I have had some local press about the Learning Tea, and let me tell you, this has never happened.

I did receive a check once for seventy-three cents. I could tell that it was from an old lady. She'd attached a sweet, handwritten note in wiggly cursive. Maybe that was all she could afford. In my mind, that will always be such a generous gift because I could tell it was a sacrifice.

As the orders stream in, I rifle through the storage room looking for my dilapidated tea box, shipped all the way from Darjeeling. It looks like it has been carried through a sandstorm on a camel's back. In the box is the better part of seventy tea packages. I've just received orders for three thousand.

I get on my computer and write a letter to my tea guy: "SEND TEA NOW!!!!!! PLEASE!!!! I'M IN DEEP SHIT."

The tea takes seventeen days to ship. We have a clause on the website that says, "Allow two to three weeks for shipping." But if you pay through PayPal, there is a mysterious window that drops down, unbeknown to me, that says, "Pay Extra: Speed Shipping, two to three business days."

It's a perfect storm. The story on Fox came out July 24, 2013. On August 7, 2013, Darjeeling goes on an indefinite tea strike. Because my tea doesn't come from some dusty warehouse in the Midwest but a genuine tea plantation that offers education to the workers' kids, I'm in a pickle. It will take at least a week to pick, dry, and package.

I immediately send out a letter to all the buyers, offering their money back and telling them the situation. After the third day, I start getting calls at my shop.

> **Me:** "Hello, Dr. Bombay's."
> **Customer:** "I want to talk to someone with the Learning Tea."
> **Me:** "Yes. This is also the Learning Tea."
> **Customer:** "Can I talk to someone in shipping?"
> **Me:** "This is shipping, how can I help you?"
> **Customer:** "I'm sorry. Actually I want the Learning Tea office manager."
> **Me:** "Yes, this is the Learning Tea office manager."
> **Customer:** "I want to talk about getting a refund or see when my tea is being shipped. Maybe I should've asked for accounting. I want to speak to accounting."
> **Me:** "Yes, this is accounting."

The first tea shipment barely came before the tea strike started. My friends, some of my staff, my dad, and I sit up until the wee hours of the morning every night for weeks wrapping, packaging, and writing thank-you notes to the people who had taken the time to invest in me and my idea. If I wasn't at work behind the counter, I was standing in line at the post office or picking up more shipping envelopes. At 2:00 AM I would start calling India to harass and bribe locals to smuggle out barrels of tea in unmarked cars to Kolkata.

After all of my friends' and family favors dried up and I couldn't afford to pay my staff for extra hours, I would stay up by myself every night, with a couple of naps, to get the last batch out. I'm beyond exhausted, a fragment of my former self. I'm glassy-eyed. I want to make people happy, and the pocket change I am making from each sale is important.

Then I get an e-mail.

"You're a fraud. I don't think you even go to India. I don't believe these girls are real. I bought tea and I want my money back. I am going to report you to the federal government."

What? I had to check a couple of times to make sure that this note was meant for me. This couldn't be a real e-mail. I am working so hard. Every minute of my day and every ounce of my being are focused on making this project work.

It is past midnight. I sit and stare at the e-mail for twenty minutes in total silence. I study every word. I fly through a range of emotions. I start crying out of exhaustion and the idea that someone could think that I was a fraud. I start worrying that other people think that, too. And then I get mad, really fucking mad.

I hate this man and his very negative attitude. I imagine him sitting at home on his fat ass writing me this threatening letter. His negativity is deflating my enthusiasm, and I'm not going to let him threaten my hard work or my girls' futures.

I write him back, and to say it was a response from a sailor would be an understatement. As I type out the last word, I click send and shoot the computer screen a double bird. I then march around my apartment celebrating and encouraging myself out loud.

"Who does he think he is, threatening me?"

About ten minutes pass, and then it hits me.

What have I done? OMG! This man is going to post this e-mail on the Internet! I'm losing my mind. I've completely lost my mind. I sit down and start to breathe deeply through my nose, trying to control my panic.

"Katrell, you are going to make it through this," I say to myself. "You have made bigger mistakes. This is not your worst screw-up. You have got to get it together. You are better than that crappy asshole. You are a nervous wreck and your reactions are whack, but you're gonna get through this."

I look around my living room and all I can see are yellow envelopes, pieces of sticky labels stuck to the walls—and my dogs. My floor is covered in lists of tea buyers that have shot out of the printer. My life is a mess. My apartment is a mess. The store is suffering. My dogs are eating the tea packaging for dinner. People are mad at me, and I need to walk away to think about my next step.

My birthday passes right by while I'm addressing envelopes. My dad sends me a birthday card with some cash stuffed inside. I decide to take a break. Maybe I'll go to a Motel 6 or to a small B&B

with a smelly cat and a doll collection. I need to find a place where I can drink, cry, and watch *Law and Order* marathons.

I am letting people down.

I go online and start looking for hotel deals. If I separate myself from this sea of packaging, I can come back recharged. I start searching for anything within driving distance. Then—from the gods themselves, or maybe William Shatner—a Travelocity pop-up window appears.

Blink, blink, blink: Five days, four nights in Las Vegas or Miami or Playa del Carmen, Mexico. Everything included!!! BUT you have to be at the gate within three hours.

I buy it, run into my room, throw a whole bunch of stuff into my suitcase, sit on the suitcase, zip it up, run out of my apartment, and race to the airport.

By 8:00 AM, I am lying on the beach in Playa del Carmen and have downed my third piña colada. An Italian men's swim team is staying at my hotel. They all have perfect Bain de Soleil tans and wear Speedos. The pool is on the top floor with a bar that wraps around it. I sit by myself at the pool for five days and four nights, downing piña coladas for breakfast. I'm wearing sunglasses and a growing smile, and I'm trying to remember to not take myself so dang seriously.

Chapter 14

EAT. SHIT. PUKE.

"Can you spare a square?"

—Julia Louis-Dreyfus
as Elaine Benes in *Seinfeld*

 ince I began traveling to India more than five years ago, I have taken more than fifty people along for the trip. Their motivations include, but are not limited to, the following:

- I'm tired of being a housewife.
- I need college credits.
- I want to find myself.
- I've heard India's weed is bitchin'.
- People are gonna be so jealous on Facebook.
- Shopping!!!!!!
- I want to find my yoga guru.
- I love tea.
- Look at me volunteering! Now let me cuss out the waiter for this chipped cup.
- If I don't go to India, I'm going to get a divorce.
- I just got a divorce.

- I want to be a Buddhist but all I have so far is a string of prayer flags from Pier 1 Imports and a rock garden water fountain I ordered on Amazon.
- I want to use your organization to make me look good.
- I just got out of rehab.
- It's cheaper than Florida, right?

Some of these have been me at one point or another. But seriously, people want to go to India for all sorts of different reasons. One thing I can say is that it's been a life-altering experience for nearly everyone who goes. And nearly all of them cry when they have to leave.

One of my friends compared traveling in India to being pregnant and giving birth: you are superexcited for it to happen; it's painful, uncomfortable, and mind-blowing while you're in the throes of it; and six months later, you want to do it all over again.

My trips to India are low on budget and high on experience. We don't do Marriott hotels or guided tours. Most of the time, we pile into hot, sweaty trains or crowd together three-to-a-room at one faded hostel or another.

On one of my trips, I bring along two curious moms from my Atlanta neighborhood. We arrive in Mumbai in the middle of the night and grab a couple of hours of restless sleep. We are staying at a huge Hare Krishna guesthouse and are awakened at 5:00 AM by cymbals, drums, and the chanting of the Krishnas doing their daily ceremony.

A few days later I am walking with Liz who has become a good friend and huge supporter of the Learning Tea. We are minding our own business, checking out the Hindu deities, when a baby monkey just below us on the hillside lets out a scream of distress. It's surrounded by a small pack of barking Pomeranian puppies that are walking with their owner off the leash.

The baby monkey's scream triggers a pack of about sixty adult monkeys who come swooping down the mountainside like something out of the *Wizard of Oz*. They reach us before they reach the baby. I take off running, but Liz freezes. I turn around and see a hulking adult baboon straddling her back. It shoves its baboon face next to her ear and bares its giant monkey teeth. A second later the baby monkey lets out another yowl and the baboon leaps from Liz's back and heads farther down the mountain. Liz looks like she's in mild shock.

I underplay it, like this stuff happens all the time. But inside I am silently chanting "Holy shit" over and over again. Before we left Atlanta, I had promised Liz's husband I would look after her. And here she is, almost devoured by a crazed baboon. There are only so many tips you can give someone, but I thought "run from monkeys" was a given. She later blames this on a snack bag I asked her to hold.

Amazingly enough, she still returns to India again and again.

※

Before every trip, there is a meeting at my shop. After all the shots have been shot and the visas have been ordered, I ask everyone to bring their fully packed bag to my shop. I go through each one and tell everyone that while they have packed for a luxurious week in the Greek isles, we are going to India. "You will be wearing the same thing for weeks, washing your clothes in a bucket of cold water," I explain. The luxury here is that there *is* water.

MY INDIA PACKING LIST

Don't overpack; you have to carry all this crap with you.
PLEASE TRY TO FIT EVERYTHING IN A CARRY-ON ONLY. You can have a backpack, bag, or purse also, but try to get your things stuffed into a carry-on. This will make things tons easier and you won't have to worry about your bags getting lost.

(YCBIT = you can buy it there)

✓ *One nice outfit to wear to meetings (Ladies, you can buy a fancy kurta there.)*

✓ *One pair of cheap rubber flip-flops (I only wear these in the shower and around the hotel.)*

✓ *One pair of slip-on sneakers. Try to find something without laces. There is poop on the ground and sometimes there isn't a place to sit to put on your shoes.*

✓ *One pair of comfortable sandals. Go for comfort, not cuteness.*

✓ *One pair of long, loose, dark-colored pants*

✓ *Two pairs of short, loose yoga pants or leggings (YCBIT)*

✓ *Two tunics (YCBIT)*

✓ *One light cover-up jacket*

✓ *One pair of long pants/pajama bottoms*

✓ *Five pairs of underwear*

✓ *Two bras*

✓ *Two pairs of socks—one for the plane*

- ✓ One bandana (YCBIT)
- ✓ One headscarf (YCBIT)
- ✓ Camera and cords
- ✓ Travel head pillow
- ✓ Business cards
- ✓ iPad mini, case, iPod
- ✓ Four-plug power converters
- ✓ Lotion
- ✓ Chapstick
- ✓ Q-tips
- ✓ Band-Aids
- ✓ Rubber bands
- ✓ Liquid soap
- ✓ Travel-size shampoo and conditioner (YCBIT)
- ✓ Deodorant
- ✓ Razors
- ✓ Toothpaste
- ✓ Toothbrush
- ✓ Pepcid AC
- ✓ Antibiotic foot cream—This is really important!
- ✓ Goody's aspirin powder
- ✓ Bug spray (nonaerosol)
- ✓ Advil
- ✓ Tweezers
- ✓ One round of antibiotics for the entire trip (one a day)

✓ Earplugs—Get some!

✓ Hand wipes or baby wipes—at least two packs. Get some!

✓ Two travel bottles of hand sanitizer

✓ Lonely Planet India book

✓ A nylon bag that folds into a tiny square—Get this!

✓ Headlamp

✓ Tiny plug-in speakers for iPad/iPod

✓ Earphones

✓ Passport

✓ Four extra passport-size pictures—You will need these!

* My India phone (You can use this whenever you want; you will just have to put money on it at the Vodafone hut on the side of the road. It's crazy cheap to call home—like four cents a minute. As soon as I get the phone turned on, everyone can e-mail the number home for emergencies.)

* Remember to contact your bank and credit card companies about the trip. Otherwise, they might suspend the card for uncharacteristic charges.

* You can usually find an Internet café to check e-mails.

* Start taking your malaria/antibiotics pills on time.

* Buy 100 percent cotton clothes because poly-blend clothes don't breathe and they soak up the scent of cow poop, incense, mothballs, and jasmine.

* Remember to relax! You are going to have an amazing time!

❋

I make sure that they have the right antibiotics, some pills to stop the vomiting, and give them the "don't eat the street food and only buy bottled water" talk. I talk a lot about water. It is hard to understate how obsessive I can be about water in India. You must plan to only drink bottled water; *never* drink from the tap, and *do not* allow others to drink from your bottle. I bring along a Sharpie that I carry in my pocket, and I tell everyone to put their initials on the bottle as soon as it's purchased. If one person gets sick, it's okay. If two people get sick, it becomes a problem. If I get sick, you're screwed. Do not even breathe near my water.

On this particular trip, there are five of us; four women and a complete dude. From the start, he doesn't listen. He wanders off and doesn't bring the right paperwork. He packs some off-white loafers and a pair of gold sunglasses. I don't know him that well, but he is struggling with a bad divorce, custody of two kids, and an apparent yearning to find his inner twenty-two-year-old suburban gangsta.

The group is a mixed bag. One of the women is still in college and on a budget, so we make a group decision that instead of spending $145 for a four-hour flight from Mumbai to Kolkata, we will instead take a third-class train for five-plus days for $8.

DAY 1–2: Dude listens to his iPod.

DAY 3: Dude complains of stomachache. We stay on the train at stops.

NIGHT OF DAY 3: Dude confesses he *might* have bought some chai from a man he saw siphoning the water out of a hose coming from inside the train.

WEE HOURS OF DAY 4: Dude is puking his guts out in train bathroom that looks like a prison bathroom in hell.

DAY 4: (Still on train) Caught the sick dude drinking out of other people's water bottles, and now everyone in the group is writhing around in their bunks, crying, puking, and stumbling to the bathrooms at both ends of the train.

DAY 4½: We get off the train and ride six hours in a 4×4 uphill into the Himalayas. Let me correct myself. It should've taken us six hours. It takes nine with all the roadside stops. There is no shame.

I know things happen; I've taken people who cannot follow rules to India. Some people who come to India are learning how to break rules, or schedules, or get away from the vicious cycle of eat, work, eat, TV, sleep. I have taken all kinds.

Sometimes I think my project is only half about helping the young women in the Learning Tea. The other half is helping people learn how to live in the moment and quit checking their Facebook.

※

We climb out of Mr. Toad's wild ride and drag our dusty luggage to our humble, paradise-in-the-sky hotel. My group is green. There cannot possibly be anything more to expel.

I throw open the door and announce our arrival to my favorite hotel, the one where I have spent months at a time. Here I will nurse my sad and dehydrated team. With a warm bed, a hot shower, and some Little League–worthy pep talks, we will be good in no time. Or at least in two to three business days.

Mr. Sonam gives me the head bobble and, without missing a beat, he says they are full.

"No rooms. All booked."

But! But! Hello!!! It's me, Katrell, your favorite guest. Miss hot chai, egg rolls with no onions. Miss I stayed in my room for nine days with no water and the curtains drawn during a political strike. Miss lady who feeds dogs. Miss I make up my own bed and reuse the same towels.

He gives me the head bobble and walks away. I turn around and see a mountain of smelly luggage and five shriveled ghost-white travelers staring at me in horror.

"Sit down. I will take care of this. Just sit down. There is the bathroom. It's gonna be okay. I'll fix this, don't worry," I say.

In India, it does no good to argue with anyone. They have already made up their mind and the only one who ends up having a coronary over the situation is you.

I'm filled with self-righteous anger. I announce that the least this completely irresponsible hotel that double-booked us can do is allow us to set up camp in the lobby. I'm venturing out to find a "decent, honest, and trustworthy place to stay," I hiss loudly.

Sara, my least-sick traveling companion, offers to come with me. She's on the tail end of her bout with death. We walk slowly up the mountain asking each hotel if they have vacancies. None do. We are defeated. I turn the bend. We venture into the next crappy hotel, curtains hanging haphazardly from the windows.

The front steps are crumbling and the lobby furniture is very loud, crackling wicker with most of the straw poking out at the bendy points. The cushions are frayed. The hanging lights are dangling lightbulbs. There's a man crawling around wiping the muddy floor with a dish towel.

"How many?" the very bossy front desk lady asks.

"Five," I say. And I nearly lose my lunch when she quotes the price. "Are you freaking kidding me?"

"Holiday," she says.

This is insane. I just saved $142 by riding a rickety and very windy train across India with no glass in the windows to spend it on a crappy hotel with no hot water, no heat, and—I know this is hard to believe—a straw bed.

"Fine, you go," she says. But I stay and try to bargain. I tell Mrs. Sherpa (I read her name tag) that I come to Darjeeling twice a year. I bring groups. I need a group price; I'm going to be here ten days. When the holiday ends and her other guests leave, I will keep paying. I'm traveling with college students looking to volunteer in her community. I go on and on, trying to tell her about my project. She doesn't care. She is ready to see this American ATM spit out money.

We are both wide-eyed, playing an exaggerated silent-movie stare-down. I turn for my friend and the door, and finally she breaks.

"Okay. You stay that long, I give you special discount."

She proceeds to give me the equivalent of thirty-nine cents off the price. She writes it on her business card with her name, writes my name on it, and circles the price over and over while she stares at me with piercing eyes.

I take the card and go to gather my deflated crew. We get two rooms, both on the bad side of awful. The beds are made from straw. The rooms are cold with no heat and no space heaters. A bluish halogen bulb hangs from a cord that sways from the draft. One bathroom has no water.

My plan is to stay here for a rest only until I can find a better option. I venture back out, sneaking through the lobby, and set out to find our forever home. After hitting eight or more hotel visits, we hit gold.

The lobby is warm. It looks clean. All the lights are on. Private bathrooms. Real mattresses. They serve hot tea in the lobby until nine. And there are rooms!

There is a nice man at the reception desk who tells me that water is available, except when Darjeeling has one of its frequent water shortages. I appreciate his honesty.

The price is not much different than the other hotel where my group is currently hunkered down.

"I'll be back. Let me just go gather my friends and I'll be back in an hour."

I am giddy as I turn on my heel to head out the door. But after the last hotel, I pause.

"Sir, can I get a look at the room?"

He hands me a key and points down the hall. Last door on the right. Number Seven.

With a bit of a touchdown dance, I hand Sara my backpack and head down the hall. What happens next is . . . hmmmmm, a car driving into a brick wall, two planes colliding in midair, a grand piano falling out of a twelve-story building window.

A thunder rises from my stomach that instantly drains every ounce of blood from my face. I almost drop to my knees. How I didn't crap my pants between that moment and running into the first room in the hall is a miracle of the gods—all of them.

I am hovering over a squat toilet. I am crying; I am in the worst pain in my life. The group wasn't kidding when they said they were sick. It is death-defying. I am rocking back and forth balanced over a white porcelain hole. My butt is uncontrollably dry heaving like a cat with a hair ball. I am sobbing, the kind where your bottom lip shakes like a kid who just fell off the slide. This goes on until I have lost at least half of my body weight.

When I finally come back to reality, I find I'm in a narrow hotel bathroom. I wipe my tears and look in the mirror. I have never looked worse. Five days without a shower. A greenish hue to my skin. And then I blink the tears from my eyes and see the toiletries. They are scattered around the sink. Little bottles of shampoo. A razor. A toothbrush and some kind of hair oil. I look out into the room and see clothes draped around the bed.

Holy crap! This is someone's room. Some poor traveler is going to walk in on this freak show any moment. I am frantically searching for toilet paper. Tissues. Anything to clean up this crime scene. I reach for the water faucet in my short-stop position. Nothing. The knob goes round and round without a drop.

There is no water to flush the toilet. I have no toilet paper. No Kleenex. Nothing. I am frantically searching for any small scrap of paper. I try to peel the labels off the little shampoo bottles.

I look like death. I have pooped on the walls. I have pooped on the floor. My butt hurts. My friend is standing in the lobby waiting, probably searching around the hotel with the receptionist to find me. She has my bag with my Kleenex and Handi Wipes. I have to clean this up and get out of here fast.

I actually start to cry nervous tears with noise that sounds like someone shaking a billy goat. And then by some miracle, I reach into my pocket and there is mean Mrs. Sherpa's business card in my back pocket from the previous hotel. Handwritten with mine and her name and her crappy discounted price circled five times.

I proceed to . . . well, let's just say the business card becomes my squeegee. I do as good of a job as I can to scrape away the evidence with the resources I have. I lay the business card in the shallow toilet basin trying to cover as much as you can cover with no water and a two-inch business card. Her name is still visible. I yank up my pants, peer down the hall toward the reception desk, and haul ass out of Room Number One. My chin is up and I am speed-walking toward the door when I hear someone calling my name.

I am face-to-face in the lobby with Mrs. Sherpa.

"This is my other hotel, why you here?" she asks.

I lie as fast as I can, surprising even myself. I might have more guests coming, I say, and was looking for more rooms.

Whether she believes me or not is beside the point.

"Okay, I check. I live here. Room Number One," she says.

Chapter 15

THE GOOD LIFE

> "Do not lose hold of your
> dreams or aspirations. For if you do,
> you may still exist but you
> have ceased to live."
>
> —Henry David Thoreau

've been leading a group of American travelers for more than a month. There's less than a week before I pick up the next set of tourists in Mumbai.

I've spent most of my time in Darjeeling sleeping in my boots, freezing my ass off, and bathing with a nearly empty package of off-brand baby wipes that I'd fished out of the sample bin at Walgreens back home. Right now, I'm in desperate need of warmer weather, so I'm heading down to South India to sit on the beach and thaw out.

I know what you are thinking: This lady goes to the beach a lot. The truth is, it's an escape—a much-needed vacation for my brain. I've seen a lot of horrific things in India, and I've been put in a lot of awful situations. I've been rattled to my core, to the point where I have wanted to run screaming to the first flight home.

Child trafficking, child labor, and infanticide, among other things, are devastating to see, and knowing that they exist burns a visual image into your brain. There are so many images I wish I could unsee. But shutting down wouldn't help anyone, so I usually go stare at the ocean for a couple of days, remember why I am here, and pull myself up by my bootstraps and dive back in.

I grab a seat on the cheapest flight to Chennai on the Bay of Bengal. Exiting the airport, I am slapped with a wall of heat. It's steamy and more than a hundred degrees.

Eyeballing long rows of white 1950s Imperials, I hop into one, and tell my taxi driver to just head down the coast.

"Just please drive until I say stop," I say. "Drive until my toes feel and look like toes again and not frozen chicken nuggets."

We weave in and out of Chennai traffic, horns blaring, dodging cows and water buffalo and jumping curbs into oncoming traffic. I don't care. The scalding breeze from the window feels wonderful. I lay my head back, soak it in, and fall fast asleep.

I wake up to feel the driver pumping his brakes to check if I am still alive. I look at my watch. Nearly two hours have passed. We are riding along the ocean. My skin is sticky with salt and sweat. The driver says something in Tamil, and I wave him onward. This may sound incredibly indulgent, but the price tag for this luxury is roughly thirty dollars.

I'm dreaming of sunny beaches, cold beer, and someone playing a sitar near an infinity pool. I slip on my sunglasses and take in the small, run-down beach hotels that pop up every few miles. There are signs with letters falling off. There are buildings that look like they're being held together by silly putty and string. My driver swings his hand out the window at every one, points, and says something. I motion for him to keep going. I'm holding out for the grand resort. If we just keep going, I know it will materialize, like an oasis.

After about thirty more minutes elapse, I can tell he's gone from nervous to very, very anxious. He eases off the gas at every sign of life, bumping along the rutted edge of the dirt highway.

I give my driver a big smile and motion on down the desolate Indian highway without a sign or light in sight.

At the next beach hotel, without a word, he whips off the road at an alarming speed. We barrel down a dirt driveway and come to a screeching halt. He jumps out of the taxi, slams the door, and runs into the reception area.

I sit in the taxi patiently. A few minutes later, he and an older woman come out of the office. He is yelling. She is mad. I get out and casually walk into the office. There are no real windows or doors. It is basically a bamboo shack with a few worn bamboo chairs. Dead marigolds are floating in a bowl of green water. I take this in and decide I will smile, listen to her sales pitch, and politely decline her offer.

The woman tells me that a local family is having a wedding party here and has rented the entire hotel, but they have one small room available above the office. I go back out with a smile to sweet-talk my driver into finding another location. When I get to the driveway, he is sitting in the car and all my things are in a big pile in the sand. As I approach the car, he locks the door, rolls down the window about one inch, puts his lips to the crack, and says something inaudible. Shaking his hand with all his fingers cinched together, I hand him a wad of rupees. Then he throws the taxi in reverse and gases it up the driveway backward. I can see his moustache quivering the entire time until I can't see him any longer. I gather up my things, beat the sand out of my sweaty travel pillow, and follow the receptionist up some dark stairs to my room.

It could be a closet. The bedroom has no windows and the mattress is made of straw.

There is a bathroom attached. The shower head hangs directly over the squat toilet. A tiny window in the bathroom looks out on a pile of broken coconut shells. The beach view is hidden by a noisy, flapping blue tarp strung from tree to tree like a sail.

I trudge back downstairs to ask for toilet paper and to see if a towel or sheets come with the room.

Sheets? She rolls her eyes. Toilet paper? This doesn't even merit a reaction. Towels? I could probably find one by the pool. Pool?! Why didn't she say so? My dilapidated, dingy beach resort catapulted from a Super 8 to a Grand Hyatt with just one word.

She warns me to stay away from the pool if the wedding guests are enjoying it.

"Don't get in their way," she scolds me, in the ever-honest Indian way.

People here do exactly what they feel. People here do exactly *how* they feel.

There is no:

"How are you?"

"Fine. Thanks."

There is:

"How are you?"

"Aww, my brother very bad sick and dying; my mother, she has bad back; my sister is mean on her cycle and I haven't been regular in days."

Any question here can bring on an onslaught of treacherous dirty laundry and family secrets. There is also brutal honesty that I have seen firsthand with fellow travelers or in other instances brought upon myself. Do not ask, "How does this look?" Because most likely you will get, "Not good, you look very fat [or very old]." This news will be delivered with a smile. I had a small boy around the age of eight run out of a ladies' undergarment store in Hyderabad to tell me he had "a very big bra to sell me."

So the pool is not mine for the taking and this is not the fabulous four-day South Indian beach and spa experience I've been dreaming about in my smelly long johns and puffy jacket for the last month. But hey, I am warm. I don't have to eat with wool gloves on, and I can *enjoy* a glass of wine and not just drink to stay warm.

I put on my thinnest kurta and some leggings and head for the beach. It is sandy and a little rocky. There are a few palm trees and cows. I stretch out my tiny pool towel amid petrified cow shit, broken flip-flops, and more fishing nets that will collect on my toes.

Every so often a wave washes in and brings more treasures— broken cell phone parts, another busted flip-flop, remnants of a broken chai cup. I dig a moat around my feet to keep it all at bay.

A man with around forty goats approaches up the beach, and I have to fight a group of them off of my book, my towel, and my hair. He laughs but doesn't stop them. When this gets old, I take my beach towel from the tug of war and head back in for a nap in my cozy, dank den.

I can see the wedding family eating a buffet of dal, lentils, rice, and a few modest-looking sweets. They are laughing. The kids are running around the pool. A cheap CD player is pumping Bollywood dance tunes, but it keeps shorting out. A bunch of moms hold naked babies in the small pool. They are wearing saris, and the bright fabric floats up around them like flower petals.

The next day I have the pool to myself for the morning. The family is building the dance floor and wedding canopy in a grassy area close to the beach. When the receptionist—who is the owner's wife—sees the kids gathering around to stare at me in my beach kurta, she quickly waves me in for a discounted spa package.

I look down at my toes and ask for a pedicure. The bright pink polish that I'd had on when I left Atlanta had been chipped away so that only a small dot remained in the middle of each toenail. She shuffles outside and speaks to an older lady bent over sweeping dirt in circles around the dirt driveway. Both of them disappear around the back of the building. Some twenty minutes pass and then the older lady comes back around the dirt road pushing a swivel office chair on wheels; one of the wheels has broken off. By the time she gets it to the front door, it is covered in dust, which she beats off with a leaf she's broken off of a low-hanging palm tree outside.

She maneuvers the chair through the front door, grunts, and firmly points for me to sit. Then she is gone again. Another twenty minutes goes by before she comes back around the corner, this time lugging a gigantic metal cooking pot filled with room temperature tap water. Some pieces of dead leaves, a few potato skins, and a wad of coconut hair are floating in the water. She slides the pot up under my feet and points again for me to put my feet in.

Then she is gone yet again. This time she comes around the corner carrying the largest pair of metal scissors I have ever seen. If they were any bigger, they'd be gardening shears.

She sits down, wraps both legs around the cooking pot, and starts working her magic. She scrapes the remaining polish off my toes with the side of one of the scissor blades and then proceeds to slowly clip my toenails while I hold my breath. I don't move an inch, balancing in my very unstable swivel office chair with a broken wheel.

After my toenails are cut, she slaps my feet, calves, and shins for a few minutes, bends my feet back and forth, wiggles them around in circles, vigorously slaps some more, and pinches each toe. Then she stands up, brushes herself off, and starts removing the pot.

I make a motion, like painting nail polish on my toes. She gives me a blank stare. I hand her money and she smiles, then totes her sloshing pot of water and the broken chair out the door and back around the corner. I am not really complaining. Some of it felt nice and the water looked clean enough. But every toenail either came to a point or there were at least three noticeable jagged hangnails.

The next night, after another rendezvous with the goat herder and his hungry brood at the beach, I settle into a chair with my swollen book, which got waterlogged while I tried unsuccessfully to wrestle it away from a goat. I fell into the ocean with it.

The sun starts to set, and all the blinking lights the family has strung in the trees around the pool and the wedding canopy begin to twinkle. The dance floor lights up this little run-down, isolated beach resort.

They roll out a gigantic buffet, turn up the music, and soon the beats start to drop. Whatever money they skimped on for the location, they make up for in the sound system. To say the music is loud would be an understatement.

Slowly, the entire family of around one hundred trickles onto the dance floor. Moms, dads, kids, aunts, uncles, cousins, second cousins, third cousins, grandpas, grandmas, all in their finest lamé and glittery saris, are whooping it up. Hands are flying, bracelets clinking, hands clapping, feet stomping on a plastic light-up dance floor wedged between sand, beach grass, and beach trash.

This goes on for three more hours while I stare. It is like a rainbow exploded. It is a full-on, turned up to eleven, Burning Man, 4:00 AM, trance-music, blasting dance festival. Everyone is chanting the chorus. Everyone is on the dance floor. This family is a jumping, moving organism full of life and glee.

Grandpas in colorful sarongs and turbans are dancing like cracked-out club kids, swinging five-year-olds up into the air. This is the true definition of "celebrate good times." I feel a twinge of jealousy at the ability for unharnessed fun with no age boundaries. It is like running onto the playground after lunch in second grade just screaming for no real reason.

I'm thinking of my Southern, sweater-set grandmother, who would barely edge a big toe onto a dance floor, and most definitely not after 8:00 PM.

One of the guests, a midthirties Indian man, sees me watching and beckons me in. I wave no, smile, and watch as he continues to dance. Later he makes his way over to my plastic beach chair. In perfect American English, he asks where I am from.

"Atlanta, Georgia, United States of America," I reply. "What about you?"

He says he was originally from a tiny town thirty miles away but now lives in San Francisco. He's come home for his sister's wedding.

"Oh, wow, San Francisco. You're so lucky. Everyone wants to live in San Francisco," I gush. "What a dream city."

He explains that he'd gotten an IT job and moved there seven years ago.

"You must love it. Great weather. Beautiful buildings. Great food. Great public transportation."

He gives me a smile out of the corner of one side of his mouth.

"It's alright," he says.

"Alright? *Eeeeeveryone* wants to live in San Francisco," I say.

I tell him again how lucky he is.

He describes his apartment that overlooks the Bay. He can see the Golden Gate Bridge from his balcony.

But his lack of enthusiasm is obvious. I figure it must be a bad boss or a little too much dancing and ask, "Hmm, well what do you do there?"

"Well, I get up, go to work, come home, eat dinner, watch TV, go to bed, get up, go to work, come home, eat dinner, watch TV, go to bed," he explains.

"Friday nights, maybe I call some friends, and Sunday night, I start complaining about going back to work, and then I do it all over again and again."

I look over his shoulder at his family, who are all undoubtedly locals. I see his grandmother throw her head back in a huge laugh, smiling with a throng of small kids dancing with one of her legs.

"You must miss this; miss your family," I say. "It must be hard; everyone looks so happy. But hey, San Francisco!"

He looks at me without batting an eye.

"You have to decide," he says, "whether you want a good life or a good lifestyle."

Chapter 16

THE CON, OR, THE HONEST BRIBE

"My name is Sylvester McMonkey McBean.
And I've heard of your troubles.
I've heard you're unhappy.
But I can fix that, I'm the fix it up Chappie.
I've come here to help you.
I have what you need. And my prices are
low and I work at great speed.
And my work is 100 percent guaranteed."

—Dr. Seuss, "The Sneetches"

 n my travels, I have come to realize that the con is a way of life in India. It's not good. It's not bad. It's expected. It's cultural. It's also a learning curve that you have to navigate around.

It shows itself in small ways, like negotiating at the market; you don't pay the asking price, and you get more respect if you're willing to banter back and forth with the shopkeeper over prices. I never negotiate if the person is selling something for less than a couple of bucks. But I will stand my ground over inflated tourist taxi fares or someone trying to dupe me on hotel rates. I've learned enough Hindi, Tamil, Bengali, and Nepali to ensure that I won't be hung out to dry or taken on a wild-goose chase around cities in a taxi.

At first, the con infuriated me. But after years of dealing with it, I refer to it as the locals do, as the "honest bribe": You know it's going to happen, so why fight it? Just ride the wave until it comes to shore and dissolves. I think most Indians find it healthy and entertaining to go back and forth with this barter system.

But it also rears its ugly head in a more serious way when you're negotiating money or opportunities. This is something I've experienced no less than fifty times in India. For me, this scenario becomes something like *Groundhog Day*; you do it over and over with different people in different locations. You hope the outcome will be different, but nine out of ten times, it ends up the same.

Here's how it might go down: You tell someone about the scholarship program you are offering, that you want to help underprivileged women have the opportunity to get an education. They agree fervently. They are onboard. They know exactly the right girls for your project in some village in some town you've never heard of or been to.

They take you out to a remote village to meet the young women. Sometimes you make ten stops along the way to visit family members who invariably need money for new stoves or furniture or to fix their tuk-tuk. They wait to see if you'll take the bait.

I've had people corral every kid in the village and tell me they are all orphans. When I didn't fall for it, I saw the kids being escorted back home by middle-class parents who had been hiding behind a nearby building. The money was never going to the kids or the families but most of the time being pocketed by the initial contact.

In the beginning, I had a bona fide organization offer to help me. They took the money for themselves, never gave it to the girls' schools, and asked me to quit visiting. When I went to the girls' families with a translator, they told me that in the meeting where I thought we'd been talking about schools, the organization had been discussing food.

There are so many brilliant, legitimate projects and people doing great things in India that I've seen firsthand. I've also had people in the United States ask me to visit projects they were sponsoring only to get there and find out the photos they were sending to their donors were staged. Maybe it was a sewing project that never existed or a water project that offered up a dirty well with nothing in it. I've made countless offers to village heads that dissolved as soon as they found out—on a trip together to the school supply store—that I pay the schools directly and they won't get a cut.

After years of letdowns, I've fine-tuned the screening questions I ask potential scholarship recipients. Here's a sampling:

- Do you live in a house?
- What is it made of?
- How many rooms does it have?
- Are you already promised to be married?
- Did either of your parents attend school?
- Does your house have electricity, running water, or a toilet?
- If you walk to get water, how far do you walk?
- Do you have both of your parents?
- What are their jobs?
- Have you ever been to the doctor?

These questions may sound intrusive, but after years of doing this, I've learned that the answers can yield a lot of clues about

whether these are the kind of girls who really need my help—
if they're answered truthfully. I've had people who translated in
interviews insist that the girls didn't speak English and presumably
feed me false answers. Then as I drive away, I hear the girls say,
"Bye, thank you so much. I really appreciate you coming for the
visit and hope to see you again soon."

It's sad the way the opportunity and situation is manipulated
to benefit the person in charge. Most of the success of the project
depends on the contact I make from the start. For every ten bad
actors, there is a redeeming burst of sunshine, a person who genu-
inely wants to get involved and really gives a damn.

On one of my trips, I had some leads from the Mother Teresa
house in Kolkata about an amazing woman who ran a "granny
rescue," as well as a small orphanage. This woman aids elderly
women who have been abandoned on train station platforms by
families who can't afford them. To have these old women spend
the rest of their lives living on the streets and begging for scraps
from commuters.

I tracked down this woman's contact information through multiple sources and she came to my hotel to meet me for tea. She told
me that she worked at a travel agency and her husband worked at
a computer shop. She was one woman collecting funds to make a
difference. She described her project, how she had rented a building where she housed some children who'd been abandoned and
paired each one of them up with a granny.

It was pretty freakin' beautiful. And she was running this on
her and her husband's tiny budget. I asked her about donations,
and she said that at the moment she was doing a donation drive
to purchase soap.

As she was talking, I remembered a granny I'd recorded on my iPhone when I'd panned around the streets of Kolkata years ago. I had seen this same frail, old woman on the same corner begging every time I'd come to Kolkata.

My new friend asked me where this woman was and I told her. She stood up and, without a word, put some rupees down on the table for our tea and walked directly out into the street, her hand up to hail a taxi. I gathered my things and ran after her. We hopped in the taxi. She didn't say a word to me, and we sped down the street toward the location I'd told her about. She jumped out of the taxi and quickly crossed the busy intersection, her colorful sari a blur.

I watched as she sat down on the street and talked to this woman, who we soon learned was blind. I want to say we put that granny in the car and drove off, but that wasn't the case. Her son, who'd been peering at us from an adjacent street corner, sauntered up with a glare and told us to back off. He explained that the granny's begging paid the bills. That is not all that unusual.

I have been friends with the granny rescue lady ever since. I have gone out to see her center, which is lovely. We meet for tea every time I'm in Kolkata and discuss our challenges. She is one of my many heroes whose work motivates me.

Let me say that the con is alive and well on the other side of the pond too. I've met a lot of people here in the United States who only want to give if someone is watching. If I say I need help stuffing envelopes or packing up items for the girls, they have no time. But if the help involves being in front of a crowd at a social function, they are first in line.

For the first time last year, I let a woman use the Learning Tea name to raise money for her travel expenses to join me in India. She came to me with a big story and a very detailed marketing plan to help me raise funds for the project. I tailored my three weeks of travel around getting her back and forth to different locations on her schedule. She loved the girls, and I thought she made a real connection. We stayed at hotels I couldn't afford and took expensive flights where I would've usually taken the train. She arrived back in Atlanta before I did, and I have never heard from her again.

The thing I've realized is that this is my passion. As much as I want to make it other people's passion as well, I just can't. It has to be their choice. They have to do it because they feel for this issue. It's not more or less important than other causes, but it's mine, and I have a personal relationship and connection with these particular girls.

Some people really get it. I've had countless folks give time and money and resources. I had a group of friends scrape together their own cash and use their precious vacation time to come to India for two weeks to help me paint, clean, and build bunk beds for one of our moves in Darjeeling. I've had a wonderful restaurant in Atlanta comp the entire bill for a fund-raising dinner at the last minute. I've had numerous college kids intern for the Learning Tea and help me complete huge, amazing projects. I've had staff from my shop come on numerous trips to India with me, who have built lasting friendships with the Learning Tea students and who really care. But the biggest lesson I've learned is that there are no limits to what you will do for your family. And these girls are my family.

Chapter 17

CLIMB EVERY MOUNTAIN

> "I guess it comes down
> to a simple choice really.
> Get busy living or get busy dying."
>
> —Tim Robbins as Andy Dufresne,
> *Shawshank Redemption*

 fter years of running the Learning Tea, I start getting pressure from others—but mostly from myself. I have to grow, multiply, get bigger, and open new centers in other cities in India. Because that's the American way.

My favorite city outside of Darjeeling is Kolkata. I love Kolkata. It's raw and moving, and if the world was a body, Kolkata would be the heart, where things are dangerous and alive and beating and everything is in the moment, where every action has a reaction and urgency and serenity all at the same time. It's survival on a minute-by-minute basis. It's insanely overcrowded and unbearably hot, and the smell is hypnotizing. In one breath you can take in incense and jasmine and livestock and diesel fuel. I have always been addicted to its chaos and feel eerily at home there.

Over the years I've learned to arrange my mandatory two trips a year in the warmer months because of my Southern intolerance to Darjeeling's harsh winters. So I usually fly to Kolkata to recoup for a couple of days before I start the long trek up to Darjeeling.

It's the opposite of Darjeeling, but the close proximity gave me hope that it would be a great location for a second center.

Kolkata is also the closest big city to Darjeeling. The overnight train leaves around 10:00 PM and arrives early the next morning in Siliguri. It's the end of the tracks at the base of the mountain, so I don't have to worry about oversleeping and missing my stop.

With its year-round warm climate, Kolkata would give me the ability to visit India in the winter months when the girls were on break from school. They could take the overnight train down and spend time with me there while escaping the winters themselves.

It would also give the girls a place to further their education goals. Darjeeling has tons of small colleges with a hundred or less students, all within walking distance of the town, but Kolkata has big universities that offer more specialized degrees and more opportunities for the girls to get acclimated to big-city life before venturing out on their own and starting careers.

Intent on expanding, I search from one end of Kolkata to the other and find a great place owned by an amazing man who was the president of one of the Kolkata Rotary Clubs. He understands my project and my goals and thinks my determination and ideas are somewhat progressive. He and his wife had been to Darjeeling to visit the project and loved it.

When I ask him about the price of the space, he says, "What can you afford?" A local Atlanta group had pledged long-term help to fund the center. I give him a price and he draws up a contract. The apartment has three bedrooms, a tidy kitchen with a built-in water filter, and a maroon fridge. There is a small, sunny balcony overlooking a playground. It is in a safe part of town.

I immediately grab all the girls who weren't currently in school that week and drag them on their first trip outside of Darjeeling to help me set up. The space has some furniture included and we purchase the other necessities.

I have a group with me from Atlanta that helps pick out some cute decorative items to make it feel homey. We hang curtains and wall coverings. And we are ready to start the interview process. I put the word out to different groups I've worked with and say that we will take five students to start with.

I want this center to focus on girls who have been involved in the sex industry and traffic victims. I interview some young ladies but most are in their late teens and have only made it to second or third grade. Most don't want to go to school but prefer a trade, like weaving or working in recycling.

There is such a big gap between rich and poor in Kolkata that they have a really hard time imagining themselves ever being a woman who works a professional job; as if they are a completely different species than the women they see in shops or the few they see working government jobs.

The second step is hiring a housemother. I set up multiple interviews. People in the community help me put out the word. I need a local woman to live there who is more than thirty years old, speaks decent English, and has some computer skills. I need her to stay in contact with me through e-mail and to send me updates and pictures. Sounds easy, right? Wrong.

What I find is a huge divide in the education and caste system. Women who have any computer skills are already living with their families or husbands in upper-middle-class houses and don't want this job. Women who could really benefit from the job have never been given a chance to use a computer or balance a checking account.

The search goes on during two different trips. I am able to spend a lot of time with the girls in Kolkata. But after an exhausting number of interviews that go nowhere and paying rent on an unused center for seven months, I give up the ghost.

I sit in the center on the last day and cry. I get on the train and cry. Then I cry some more at my hotel. All the meetings and contacts it took to get me to this place. All the time spent in hot cars driving around looking at dead-end spots. All the networking events I'd attended, convincing people to give this idea a chance. All the potential landlords that said no when they realized a man wouldn't be signing the lease. All the trips to get the best kitchen supplies for the cheapest prices, the hours of deep-cleaning the maroon fridge where I'd discovered moldly meat. The one-day event of finding a hammer and nails to hang up the tapestries, and all the girls I could've helped if I'd just had more time and resources.

The Atlanta group found another project to back, one that gave their website a bigger bang for the buck and had more bragging rights. They don't understand that things take time in India, that getting this off the ground is a process. So I have failed, and I have to go back to Atlanta with my tail between my legs because I couldn't make this happen.

I arrive home feeling defeated, trying not to think about Kolkata. I don't want to talk about it when people ask. "No, the center didn't succeed. Yes, I had to close it."

I try to concentrate on the small victories. Sometimes it's one step forward and two steps back. I remind myself that I haven't failed. The love remains, which, to me, is the key to the success of this project. It's behind every day and every action the girls and I take. This project is not about an amount of money that sits in a bank. For the girls, it's knowing that there's a lifetime of support and a family when most of them had none. It's encouragement from me and their peers and the housemother. It's having someone help with homework and hairdos. It's having someone ask how your day went or all of us packing for a day hike or a trip to the zoo or the movies. It's them waking up and knowing that there is a whole group of people on this planet who love them and care that they exist. For me, it's knowing that I have made some kind of difference, however small. And like my grandfather taught through his actions, one tiny seed can grow a garden of change.

My spirits are lifted by e-mailing the girls, sending photos of the trip, and getting updates—my shiny bit of sunshine. The first e-mail I usually receive from them when I return to Atlanta almost always includes, "When are you coming back? Have you booked your tickets for your next trip?"

But one day at work I get an e-mail from Angel that pops up on my phone. The subject line jumps off the screen at me because it says she needs money. Neck-deep in flour, I'm caught off guard.

This has never happened. Not one of these girls has ever asked for money for anything frivolous—not clothes or shoes or any electronic gadget.

I purchase clothing while I'm there, and they get haircuts every six months. I take them to the eye doctor and update their glasses. We buy shoes and new winter coats if needed. We have a system that any expenses have to be okayed thirty days before the amount is due. This gives me time to raise money or shuffle around funds in my store account. Immediately worried, I brush off the flour and open Angel's e-mail.

Angel was the fifth girl in the program. I brought her younger sister into the house six months before she arrived. On the next visit, I was told about her by her sister. Even though Angel was older, she was behind in school. Her mother was a domestic servant who lived with the family she worked for.

Angel lived in a village on the outskirts of town by herself in a little shack made from corrugated metal tacked together. Due to malnutrition and a severe iron deficiency, she was unable to use both of her legs and couldn't walk up the steep road, so she was out of school for close to two years.

When she first came to the house, she was really skinny and extremely skittish. I think she thought the rug was going to be ripped out from under her at any moment. Now she's taller than any of the other girls. She has a very soft, whispery voice that sounds raspy at times. Her smile lights up the room and she can be a real ham. When the girls began watching *High School Musical*, she learned every word and dance move within days. She asked me if I knew Zac Efron. A natural athlete, she is now on the volleyball team.

Steeling myself for bad news, I open the e-mail:

Hello Tiger Heart,

It's Angel here. Hope you are well. I have been elected to train for trekking up Mt. Everest. I have been selected to be one of 12 girls with 1,500 girls competing. I will need money for trekking supplies. I will be going to base camp next month if you say yes.

I can do this.

We are very much missing you.

Your girl,

Angel

With a smile that I cannot contain, I sit down to type my reply.

In February 2015, Angel began her climb.

Epilogue

At some point in my life, I don't know when I saw it, maybe on a coffee cup, I remember reading the quote that I put in the beginning of the book: "I slept and dreamt that life was joy, I awoke and saw that life was service, I acted and behold service was joy."

Writing about my time in India brings it all before me once again in lucid detail: I am writing this now, a few months after the book's due date, sitting at my kitchen table in New Orleans. It's been a rocky road, collecting my life into 50,000 words. All the small details of my life coming into color on paper. Remembering the smells and intensity of my first trip to India. Arranging details in my mind, like setting a table for dinner and then when everyone is about to sit down, remembering the salad fork or the spoon goes on the left. I would write something I thought was a fantastic memory only to sit back and wonder if people would even care. The details that get lost in my memory of the event. The smell of cardamom in the bottom of a cup of chai tea, the small breeze from a heavy burqa as it brushes against my leg on a train seat, the haze of an Indian morning with kids giggling far off in the distance in a rice field at a train stop in the middle of nowhere.

On my first trip to India, traveling from Hyderabad to Darjeeling, I stopped in Kolkata on the way. At my hotel there was an array of misspelled pamphlets in the lobby: "Kolkata home of Mother Theresa," "Kolkata home of Kolkata Knights cricket team." "Go see the world largest banyan tree," and on the smallest worn leaflet, it said, "Visit the home of Rabindranath Tagore who died in 1941 and was a Bengali poet, writer and artist from Kolkata."

I did go see the world's largest banyan tree, and I've visited most tourist attractions with groups I've brought on my trips through Kolkata. But one morning I left the beaten path and decided to visit Rabindranath Tagore's house. On the leaflet was a sketch of an old Raj-style home that looked enchanting, and the description accompanying it said that I could tour the home and visit the garden and bookstore/gift shop.

The house was down a narrow alleyway, so the cab driver said he would wait for me on the next street over. The house was big and the courtyard was dotted with manicured fruit trees. Tagore was a poet from West Bengal who left his home to find the world outside of Kolkata; in the process, he found himself. I saw his bed with white covers where he died and his mother's room, where his framed poems hung. I then headed down to the gift shop and purchased a small pile of notebooks for my friends back home.

When I got back to my hotel and was packing up for the next leg of the trip, I wrapped the gifts in a T-shirt. I flipped through the pages of one of them, and on the last page of one dusty little notebook was the quote that I started this book with: "I slept and dreamt that life was joy, I awoke and saw that life was service, I acted and behold, service was joy" (Rabindranath Tagore). The Buddha said that there are no coincidences. I tore the page out and carried it with me, reading it a few hundred times. I taped it to the backside of my apartment door and then moved it to a corkboard that hung over my desk. On one of my moves, it was lost in the shuffle, but it didn't matter, because I had read it so many times, I had memorized it.

I know tattoos are not for everyone (especially my dad), but I have them. I have a Georgia dogwood branch running up one arm and onto my back. On it sits two wrens because my dad and grandfather are both named Ren. I have paisleys, which were on the first Learning Tea logo, patched in around the branches.

All the tattoos are nicely hidden with a long-sleeve kurta or button-down shirt at business meetings. I've made sure to keep them above the cuff of a rolled-up sleeve. Sometimes I get a chance to explain why I have them, but they also serve as a reminder that this project is a lifelong commitment.

I've saved a spot on the inside of my upper arm for the Tagore quote. After my first trip to India, where I met the future Learning Tea students, I made an appointment for my tattoo. I had a month to get the quote translated from English to Bengali, like

I wanted. Seems easy, right? Wrong. Trying to find the written Bengali script in the midst of my travels in India—and all I was pursuing there—was always at the forefront of my mind, so much so, that it had become a joke with my staff at the shop, the people I'd taken to India, the interns for the Learning Tea, and my friends. That quote is my Holy Grail, my Bigfoot, my Loch Ness monster.

It was originally written in Bengali by Tagore then transcribed into English, and it's a small piece of a larger work. If you ask someone to transcribe it, they give it to you in English letters, not in Bengali script. If you ask someone to find it in Bengali, they can't; they say it is lost in his written works that live in Kolkata.

I've asked scholars at his home to find it, but to no avail. I've asked for help at the Tagore Institute, but they didn't have it in Bengali. Speaking Bengali is common in Kolkata but writing the script seems to be a lost art. You can look it up on the Internet, but it spits it back to you in English. If you click on "translate in Bengali lettering," the translation is muddled and comes back saying something else and backward. I had the mother of an Indian volunteer in the states do a transcription, but she did it in Hindi, not Bengali.

During this quest over the last five years, I've been to the Tagore house four times, have asked countless Bengalis about it, and had friends work on it for fun, but the search has remained elusive.

Then, one day—a day I was supposed to have off—my life took a different direction when a man named Thanh Truong walked into my shop. He had been living down the street for years, but, as luck would have it, he was moving in three days for a job in New

Orleans. It didn't seem to matter. We became inseparable.

After a year of shuttling back and forth between Atlanta and New Orleans, Thanh and I were married on a fishing boat in the Mekong River in midafternoon on a Thursday by a boat captain who was our only witness. My dress was one I had found a few weeks earlier in the "free" bin in Kolkata, and I carried a bouquet of hydrangeas we had bought at a roadside flower stall.

With a great staff and an amazing business partner, I am able to go back and forth to New Orleans for a few weeks (carting my dogs with me on the seven-hour drive), then back to Atlanta to work at the shop while my business partner takes off.

Atlanta is my home; I've had the same group of friends for ten-plus years, whereas New Orleans is uncharted territory for me. It's been hard, moving away from everything I know and love, to start a new life. And while I've joined a book club and volunteer in the area, at times I wonder how I got here and if I'm on the right path. Sometimes I think, *Yes, I'm with the man of my dreams, but what am I doing here?*

One night in New Orleans I called a cab from an app on my phone. The driver picked me up, and before I told him the directions to our new apartment, I asked how he was, and he responded with "Palo ache." That's Bengali for "I am good." It took me a second, and then we were in deep conversation about Kolkata. He told me that New Orleans was the Kolkata of the United States. Just like the Hooghly River often flooded Kolkata, the same was true of the Mississippi in New Orleans. At any moment, both cities could get a big rain and the streets would be filled with water. He said that New Orleans was gritty like Kolkata and had its fair share of characters. Both cities had lots of street food and many festivals with parades (in fact, New Orleans is known as the "Festival Capital of the World") and regarded the arts as the highest form of education. Both cities were hot and sometimes smelly, but the people were "most friendly." He told me that his wife and daughter still live in Kolkata, and that he sends money back to them each month. I told him I would love to talk more sometime, and I saved his number in my phone.

A few months later, I remembered him and started searching for the "driver from Kolkata" in my phone list. I might be the only one who has this problem, but I have seven or eight numbers I've saved with the title of "driver from Kolkata." Soon after, I sent out a text: "Are you the driver who drives for United Cabs in New Orleans, Louisiana, United States of America, that is from Behalla neighborhood in Kolkata, India?"

I didn't receive a response from anyone. I waited a week and then started calling the numbers. After the third attempt, a man answered yes, it was him; he hadn't answered initially because he thought the text was a scam. I asked him if he wanted to go to lunch with me and my husband, and he said he would pick us up in twenty minutes.

"No, I don't need a ride. I wanted to know if you wanted to go to lunch," I said. He said he would come to pick us up after lunch if I called him then.

I said, "No, we want you to sit with us; we don't need a taxi."

He said, "You want me to not pick you up but come in and wait with you for you to eat your lunch?"

I said, "No, I want to meet you at the restaurant and eat lunch as friends, and I will buy your lunch, but we do not need a ride."

Then he told me he couldn't, that he had too many food restrictions to eat out and said we should get together another time. He told me he ate at the Indian temple in New Orleans every day. I told him that I would also like to eat at the Indian temple in New Orleans and tried to worm my way into his schedule. He said, "Fine, tomorrow we meet at the temple for lunch at one," and then he texted me the address.

The next day I put on a nice kurta and my fanciest flip-flops and headed for the temple, which happened to be a short distance from my apartment in New Orleans. When I drove up, the temple was in a huge, old New Orleans–style house. There were United taxicabs lined up around the streets. Inside there were some tables with paper plates; one table was set up with a paper tablecloth. They told me that the house once belonged to a ship captain.

My driver, Mr. Rau, asked if I wanted to see the temple before we ate, because it was getting ready to close until the next service. We went out the door from the basement, around to the front of the house, climbed up the ten or so stairs, and then inside the front door. I quickly slipped off my shoes. We walked around a few halls and then down another flight of stairs. As I was following him, I got a whiff of India. The smell is like no other place; it's salty and sweet, like their chutney. Then the room opened up. It was beautiful, all hardwood walls and ceiling, no chairs, no windows, and an entire wall covered with sparkly, life-size Hindu gods, with spotlights pointed on each one for a mesmerizing effect. I felt the cold tile floor under my feet.

There was an Indian lady shuffling around in a gold and burgundy sari, a cute, chubby baby crawling around on the floor, and, in the corner, a little sadhu (holy man) writing on some papers on a straw mat. This room was India, not a New Orleans version of India. The sadhu could've been from the banks of the Ganges. He was wearing a sarong tucked in the front and nothing else. He had dark skin shining with sweat from the hot room. He had a plethora of beads hanging from his neck. He looked up and gave us a welcoming nod. Mr. Rau asked for a blessing, and the sadhu put a little silver can on my head, said a few things, and then handed me a plate that looked like some dried-out yard cuttings, and I took a pinch to nibble on.

We went up the stairs and back around the corner to the room with the food. We sat down and were served a delicious meal of dal, rice, chapatti, and chutney. There was cool lemon water to drink. The sadhu came in, and I waved him over to sit with us. Through his very broken English, we talked about India and Kolkata. I showed him photos of the Learning Tea on my phone, and the rest of the cab drivers came over to see the pictures. Mr. Rau apologetically said he had to get back to work.

"You are family now. Come anytime; you are from Kolkata and we are also from Kolkata; we are all Indian family," said Mr. Rau, and then all the cab drivers shuffled out the door. I finished up my last bites of dal with the sadhu. We sat looking at my photos and I asked him about the temple. It had been in New Orleans for forty years. I told him how much it made me homesick for India, the food, and the smells. I asked him how they got their financing to maintain such a big house in New Orleans, and he told me that they had Indian donors from all over the world. He told me he lived there full-time and did two services a day. Making small talk, I asked him if he did anything else with his time.

He said, "Yes, I am a Bengali transcriber."

I wrote my little quote on a piece of paper from my purse and handed it to him. He smiled and said, "Ah, Tagore, I know it very, very well. Come by tomorrow and you can pick it up."

$\mathcal{A}$ $\mathcal{N}$ote on the Learning Tea

As my project has grown, I've given a lot of thought to how it should evolve.

It began with a fishbowl on my counter at the tea shop collecting spare change. It's now funded, in part, through monthly Indian dinners at my shop and the sale of packages of Darjeeling tea, as well as small donations from individuals and a community musical/yoga festival.

But the main source of money is my shop, Dr. Bombay's.

Dr. Bombay's monthly dinners are run by volunteers. Most of them have been to India at least once. The dinners give the community a fun place to come together and meet new friends. It also gives the volunteers the opportunity to stay engaged and tell other people about the project. This is how I have met some of my greatest supporters who have traveled with me on different trips and have stayed very invested in the girls' futures.

I look up to big social enterprises or businesses that give back, like TOMS (Shoes), Patagonia, and Newman's Own, and I think a lot of businesses are moving in this direction. When I'm spending my own money, I seek out businesses and products that support social justice and human rights' issues. I am proud to be a social entrepreneur, where supporting businesses that support a cause goes a long way. I love that my neighborhood sees the value in giving back through their purchases.

It's important to me to have a dependable, steady stream of income for this project. It makes me feel safe with the growth and expenses we have in Darjeeling. When we say scholarships, we mean life scholarships. They cover the big things like education, living expenses, and medical bills but also the small stuff like music lessons, winter coats, and the occasional Band-Aid.

A lot of Americans already grab a coffee or tea a few times a week. My customers just choose to grab it at my place. And there is a lot of power in that purchase. I want to stretch that dollar with my project and use it for good. My staff and I know that while we are serving tea, we are also creating change and opportunity. And that makes our sweets that much sweeter.

Visit: *www.drbombays.com* and *www.thelearningtea.com*.

How You Can Help the Learning Tea

Thank you for your interest in supporting the Learning Tea! A portion of the proceeds of this book will go toward our program, and every little bit of help we get goes a long way in the lives of our scholars. Here are some of the ways to help:

- **Purchase Learning Tea online.** Packs of Learning Tea help fund necessities like notebooks, book bags, and shoes. Black and green teas are available and we are currently working on a great new line of tea. *www.thelearningtea.com.*

- **Donate air miles.** We love getting air miles! Flying to India is one of our greatest expenses and air miles are a huge help. Delta SkyMiles can be donated to Katrell Christie's account; please see the web site for details.

- **Join us on a trip to India.** We only go to India twice a year, so we have to get the most out of every trip. The more manpower we have the more we can get done! This is the most hands-on way you can help. For more information visit *www.thelearningtea.com* and go to the "India Trip" tab.

- **Follow us and spread the word.** Follow the Learning Tea and Dr. Bombay's Underwater Tea Party on Facebook, Twitter, Pinterest, and Instagram for daily information about events and other ways that you can support our scholars.

- **Drink and dine at Dr. Bombay's Underwater Tea Party.** The store is a huge part of how we spread the word about our work, and you can easily support the cause by making a donation at the store.

- **Attend our monthly "A Taste of India" dinners, or volunteer at one of them.** Our dinners take place on the last Monday of each month at 6:30 PM. For a $20 ticket, you can enjoy an authentic Indian three-course vegetarian meal. You can also purchase a raffle ticket for $1 to enter a chance to win a fantastic basket full of unique treasures. All of the proceeds of our dinner go directly to our scholars.

About the Coauthors

Katrell Christie is the founder and owner of the Learning Tea, a project which helps provide schooling and a safe haven for impoverished young women in India. Through her efforts, she has helped to change the lives of many women.

Shannon McCaffrey is an award-winning reporter and editor for the *Atlanta Journal-Constitution*. She is an avid reader, mother, and a runner.

My boat on the Ganges River.

The July 2009 eclipse over Varanasi, India.

The crowd on the ghats of the Ganges River.

My great friend Cate.

Loading our garden crates into the tuk-tuk.

Zabeers helping shovel dirt for our garden project.

The altar decorated to celebrate the goddess Lakshmi.

Setting up our garden project.

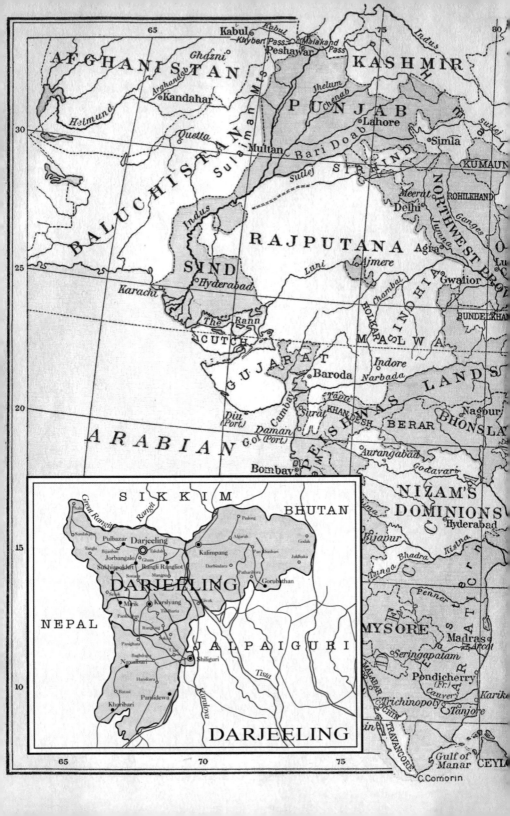

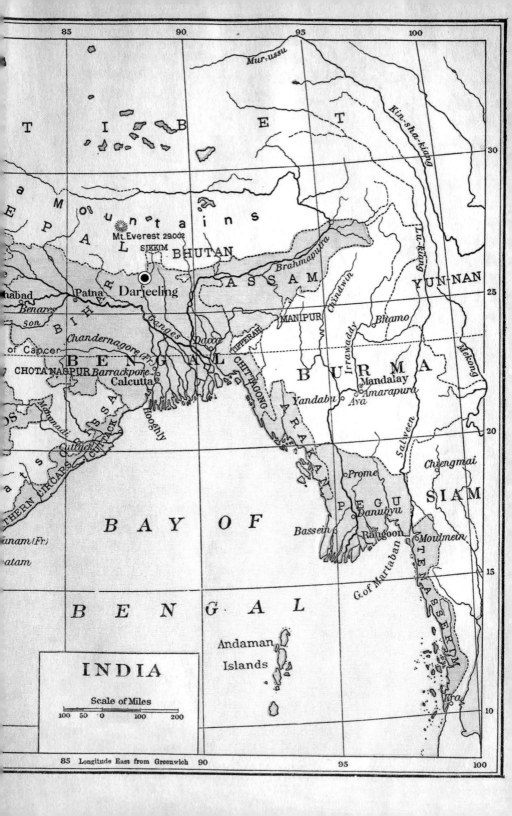

85   90   95   100

Mur:ussu

T I B E T

30

Kin-sha-kiang

M O U N T A I N S

Mt.Everest 29.002
SIKKIM   BHUTAN

Brahmaputra

A S S A M

YUN-NAN

25

●Darjeeling

Chindwin

Patna

Ganges

MANIPUR   *Bhamo*

Chandernagore(Fr.)

Dacca

B E N G A L

TIPPERAH

CHITTAGONG

B U R M A

CHOTA NAGPUR *Barrackpore*

Calcutta

Mandalay

Yandabu   *Amarapura*
Aya

Hooghly

A R A K A N

Salween

20

Chiengmai

Prome

S I A M

P E G U

Danubyu

B A Y   O F

Bassein   Rangoon

Moulmein

T E N A S S E R I M

15

G.of Martaban

B E N G A L

Andaman
Islands

INDIA

Scale of Miles
100 50 0   100   200

Kra

10

85 Longitude East from Greenwich 90   95   100

Winding through the mountains to reach Darjeeling.

Village children.

Darjeeling tea gardens.

Houses in
the hills.

A chai stop on our
trek into the mist.

Me and one of the students.

The Learning Tea scholars.

Our living room before we moved to Up-Up road.

A student in her uniform.

Spices in Kolkata.

On one of our trips to Kolkata, the girls picked out books to take back to Darjeeling.

The Learning Tea scholars channeling their inner "Tiger Hearts."

Me and the girls outside
of the center.

Our first Learning Tea
sign we had painted
on Up-Up road.

My Roller Derby photo as Takillya Sunrise.

#1800

Takillya Sunrise

Hanging out at my tea guy's shop.

Me and our tea.

*Our evening
dinner and chat.*

*Angel in her
mountaineering gear.*

Angel training for her climb.

Angel with her trekking group.

Me and Thanh picking out our wedding flowers at a market stall in Vietnam.

The first photo of the married couple.

An "only in India" story—we told you there was a monkey riding a pig!